Marketing Research

Project Manual

James Molinari
State University of New York at Oswego

McGraw-Hill Irwin

Boston   Burr Ridge, IL   Dubuque, IA   Madison, WI   New York
San Francisco   St. Louis   Bangkok   Bogotá   Caracas   Kuala Lumpur
Lisbon   London   Madrid   Mexico City   Milan   Montreal   New Delhi
Santiago   Seoul   Singapore   Sydney   Taipei   Toronto

McGraw-Hill
Irwin

MARKETING RESEARCH PROJECT MANUAL

Published by McGraw-Hill/Irwin, a business unit of The McGraw-Hill Companies, Inc., 1221 Avenue of the Americas, New York, NY, 10020. Copyright © 2006 by The McGraw-Hill Companies, Inc. All rights reserved. No part of this publication may be reproduced or distributed in any form or by any means, or stored in a database or retrieval system, without the prior written consent of The McGraw-Hill Companies, Inc., including, but not limited to, in any network or other electronic storage or transmission, or broadcast for distance learning.

Some ancillaries, including electronic and print components, may not be available to customers outside the United States.

This book is printed on acid-free paper.

1 2 3 4 5 6 7 8 9 0 QPD/QPD 0 9 8 7 6 5

ISBN 0-07-312888-0

Editorial director: *John E. Biernat*
Publisher: *Andy Winston*
Sponsoring editor: *Barrett Koger*
Editorial assistant: *Jill M. O'Malley*
Executive marketing manager: *Dan Silverburg*
Lead project manager: *Mary Conzachi*
Senior production supervisor: *Sesha Bolisetty*
Design coordinator: *Cara David*
Lead media project manager: *Cathy L. Tepper*
Developer, Media technology: *Brian Nacik*
Cover design: *Brian Perveneckis*
Typeface: *10/12 Times Roman*
Compositor: *GTS—New Delhi, India Campus*
Printer: *Quebecor World Dubuque Inc.*

Library of Congress Cataloging-in-Publication Data
Molinari, James M.
 Marketing research project manual/James M. Molinari.—1st ed.
  p. cm.
 ISBN 0-07-312888-0 (alk. paper)
 1. Marketing research—Handbooks, manuals, etc. I. Title.
HF5415.2.M625 2006
658.8'3—dc22
                                        2005041500

Marketing Research

Project Manual

*To my wife Beth and our children Tim, Steve and Sara; and to my
parents Joseph and Sara Molinari*

Contents

preface   *viii*

Chapter 1
The Marketing Research Project   1

Introduction   1

Project Overview   1

Major Steps in the Marketing Research Process   2

Step 1: Review the Decision Situation and Define the Problem   3

Step 2: Define the Research Objective and Information Needs   3

Step 3: Select a Research Design   3

Step 4: Design the Research Instrument   4

Step 5: Determine the Sample Plan   4

Step 6: Collect and Process the Data   4

Step 7: Analyze and Interpret the Data   4

Step 8: Present Research Findings to Decision Makers   4

Appendix 1A: Forming Your Group   5

Appendix 1B: Marketing Research: Peer Evaluation   7

Appendix 1C: Score Sheet: Marketing Research Project   9

Chapter 2
Choosing a Topic   11

Introduction   11

Customer Satisfaction Studies   11

Market Segmentation Studies   12

Concept Testing   12

Customer Attituds and Usage Studies   13

The Client   14

The Assignment   15

The Group Meeting   15

What to Submit   15

Chapter 3
Review of the Decision Situation   17

Introduction   17

Decision Situation   17

The Assignment   18

Situation Analysis   18

Company Analysis   19

Customer Analysis   19

Competitor Analysis   20

Sources   20

Chapter 4
Research Objectives and Information Needs   21

Introduction   21

Decision Situation   21

Decision Problem to Research Objectives   22

Information Needs   23

The Assignment   24

Chapter 5
Literature Review   27

Introduction   27

Conceptual Definition   28

Methodology   28

Measures   29

Determinants of Customer Satisfaction/ Segmentation Variables   29

The Assignment   30

Sources   30

Notes   30

Chapter 6
Methodology   31

Introduction   31

Primary Data Collection Methods   31

Questioning Methodology   32

Question Format   33

Getting Cooperation   34

The Assignment   34

Primary Data Collection Methods   34

Chapter 7
Questionnaire Design   35

Introduction   35

The Process   35

Determine What Information You Need   36

Determine the Method of Administration and Questionnaire Type   36

Determine the Content of Individual Questions   36

Determine the Form of the Response to the Question   36

Decide on the Wording of Each Question   38

Determine the Question Sequence   39

Determine the Layout   39

The Assignment   41

Chapter 8
The Sampling Plan   43

Introduction   43

Population   43

Sampling Frame   44

Sampling Procedure   44

Sample Size   45

Sample Size Determination When Estimating Means   45

Sample Size Determination When Estimating Proportions   46

The Assignment   48

Chapter 9
Coding and Data Entry using SPSS   49

Variable View   51

Variable Names   51

Variable Type   51

Variable Label   52

Value Label   52

Measurement Level   52

Entering Data   53

Chapter 10
Basic Data Analysis   55

Measurement Scales   55

Descriptive Statistics   56

Charts   57

Cross-Tabulations   58

Transforming Variables   60

Recoding a Variable   61

Summary   61

Chapter 11
The Written Report   63

Format of the Written Report   63

Title Page   64

Table of Contents   64

Executive Summary   64

Introduction: Review of the Decision Situation   64

Body   65

Data Analysis and Findings   66

Conclusions   66

Limitations   66

Appendixes   66

A Few Final Thoughts   66

Studying marketing research should be an interesting and rewarding experience that provides students with opportunities not only to learn about marketing research but also to gain a valuable perspective on marketing decision making.

This manual is intended for students taking their first course in marketing research who have as a major requirement of the course the design of a marketing research project. It initially was developed to serve as a guide for students enrolled in my marketing research class, which is a required course in the marketing curriculum. This manual has been classroom tested and revised on the basis of student feedback and modified to be an appropriate guide for most marketing research courses that require an applied marketing research project.

This project manual has been designed to guide you in a step-by-step manner as you proceed through the semester. A problem that cuts across all student research projects stems from the reality of the academic semester, which is too short to allow the project to begin after the student has received instruction in all phases of the research process. Students are asked to design a research study as they are learning content material and before they have been exposed to all the concepts and methodologies they ultimately will need to utilize. While this approach effectively reinforces the material covered in class and in the text, it inevitably is a source of frustration for the students, who rarely feel that they have the "big picture." As a result, students have a number of very pragmatic questions at each stage of the research process, questions that are not fully addressed in the text. This manual attempts to anticipate and answer those questions and is the result of thousands of meetings held with individual students and student groups. It is intended to complement a standard text and to be a resource that can be consulted periodically as you progress from one stage to the next of the research project.

This manual has been designed around a typical student project. Your instructor has determined that the best way to learn marketing research is by doing it. As is the case with students studying marketing research at universities across the country and around the world, your project will require the design and implementation of a marketing research study. While the type of study will vary from group to group, the process that each student group will follow will be very similar. This manual has been designed to guide you through that process.

I believe that you will find this project to be a challenging yet rewarding experience. You will be developing new skills as well as new ways to think about marketing problems. You will gain insight into the field of marketing research and acquire an appreciation for the many potential pitfalls that face a typical marketing research study. As a future user of marketing research, you will gain a greater appreciation for the methodologies that are required to produce valid, action-oriented findings.

It is my hope that this manual answers your questions and provides insights that enhance your understanding of marketing research. Good luck!

James M. Molinari
State University of New York at Oswego
January 2005

I want to thank Dean Lanny Karns for his support of my efforts, as well as the many students who have asked the questions that were the catalyst for this manual. Thanks are also due to the efforts of Jill O'Malley and Barrett Koger of McGraw-Hill, whose support and encouragement were critical for transforming an idea into the successful completion of this manual. I am also indebted to the following reviewers for their thoughtful and helpful comments and suggestions: David Mick, University of Virginia; Steven Moff, Pennsylvania College of Technology; Michael Hyman, New Mexico State University; Paul Sauer, Canisius College; Lisa Toms, Southern Arkansas University; Brooke Quigg, Pierce College; De'Arno De'Armond, West Texas A&M University; Felicia Lassk, Northeastern University; Tom Baker, University of North Carolina; Scott Swain, Boston University; and Ron Dickinson, University of Maryland University College.

CHAPTER 1

The Marketing Research Project

Introduction

This manual has been written to guide you through the various steps and stages of your marketing research project. It will provide some answers to and insights into many of the questions that you will have as you apply the concepts and ideas of the marketing research course to an applied marketing research project.

Applying the concepts you will learn in class by conducting a marketing research project will be a rewarding, sometimes frustrating, but in the end a worthwhile experience that will allow you to gain valuable insight into the role of marketing research in the real world. You will develop and refine a number of skills during the course of the semester; this can occur only as a result of a hands-on marketing research project.

Since you will be engaged in a real-life project, learning will be experience-based and probably will become more internalized than would learning associated with reading a text. As in any experience-based learning situation, the learning that occurs will be learner-based and dependent on the effort and involvement of the individual student. Your instructor has determined that the best way to learn marketing research is by doing it. At universities across the country and around the world, students like yourself will design and implement a marketing research project.

The nature of these studies will vary greatly. Some will be focused on small businesses in the vicinity of campus, others will deal with on-campus agencies or local not-for-profits, and still others will be studies for large national or global businesses. The type of study will vary as well, from customer satisfaction studies to concept tests for new products, brand awareness studies, or any number of studies typically conducted to assist marketing decision makers.

The methods you will utilize over the course of this semester will depend on the nature of your project and the questions you need to answer. This manual has been developed as a result of working with hundreds of student groups over a wide range of research projects. It will offer insights into the research process and suggest questions you will need to consider as you proceed. The direction that your project follows, however, will result from your decisions.

While each marketing research project is unique, the issues addressed by most student groups are very similar. This manual is intended to help guide you throughout the process. Good luck!

Project Overview

You will be a member of a project team, whose size will be determined by your instructor. Each team is responsible for the design of a detailed marketing research project. It is likely that your assignment will include all the steps associated with a marketing research study; however, in some cases data collection will be based on smaller samples than would usually be the case in order to accommodate the time and budget constraints associated with student projects. Every marketing research problem is unique in some way, and each project requires customized solutions and approaches. Still, there is a standard sequence of steps, called the *research process,* that can be used in any research study. While your instructor will provide specific instructions regarding the nature and scope of your assignment, this manual will take you inside the research process to help guide you at each step and provide some insights that should help you produce an effective project that meets the needs of your client and provides you with an outstanding learning experience.

The project itself will place you and your teammates in the role of a small marketing research company. You will be working on a project for a "client"; an individual, agency, firm, or organization that can benefit from a marketing research study. Your instructor probably will allow you to select your own client. If you are having difficulty identifying a cooperative client, your instructor will be able to help you since local businesses regularly contact universities with requests for student projects.

Throughout the semester, your instructor will serve as an adviser, answering questions that are not covered in this manual or in the text. Remember, however, that this is your project. The important decisions and the responsibility for carrying out each step of the project are yours. While the project will require a significant effort and a lot of hard work, alumni regularly report the experience as one of the most meaningful and memorable of their academic careers.

The team is to assume the following situation: You represent a marketing research firm that has been asked to submit a detailed marketing research study to a potential client. The client has asked that the project include the following components:

1. A review of the decision situation
2. A review of the relevant literature of published studies to confirm your familiarity with current practice
3. A detailed breakdown of research objectives and information needs
4. A detailed plan for the data collection procedures you intend to use
5. A questionnaire
6. A sampling plan
7. Data analysis
8. A budget
9. Résumés for each member of the team

Your instructor will evaluate your work on the basis of the quality of the project, which includes the components listed above as well as the content and means of presentation of the written materials with regard to spelling, sentence structure, and so on.

You will be completing an entire project study from start to finish. Such a project requires a series of steps, each of which is detailed in your textbook and will be covered in class. Your instructor may require that you hand in each stage of the project by a designated date to provide you with the opportunity to benefit from instructor feedback. Make sure to take advantage of the process by seeking out as much feedback as possible.

A problem that cuts across all student research projects stems from the nature of the academic semester, which is too short to allow the project to begin after you have received instruction on all phases of the research process. You will be asked to design a research study as you are learning the content and before you have been exposed to all the concepts and methodologies you will ultimately need to utilize. While this approach effectively reinforces the material covered in the text and in class, it is a potential source of frustration for students who may not feel that they have the "big picture" regarding the project requirements. This manual is the result of thousands of meetings with individual students and student groups. It draws on those meetings to anticipate the areas of confusion or the questions that generally arise and offers insights and suggestions that should help make this project assignment an enjoyable and rewarding experience.

Major Steps in the Marketing Research Process

Every marketing research project is unique in some way, requiring a customized approach designed to address the specific situation facing the decision maker. The *marketing research process* is a series of interrelated steps, with each step having an impact on the others. The research process is described in your text in detail. While texts differ somewhat with regard to the language used to describe the process, the process generally is presented as a series of steps similar to those below:

1. Review the decision situation and define the decision problem.
2. Define the research objective and information needs.
3. Select a research design which includes the following steps:
   a. Identify data sources.
   b. Identify the data collection method.
4. Design the research instrument.
5. Determine the sample plan.
6. Collect and process the data.
7. Analyze and interpret the data.
8. Present research findings to decision makers.

Step 1: Review the Decision Situation and Define the Problem

Before marketing research can provide any useful insights, it needs to help define the problem to be solved. Usually the decision maker has a sense of the problem and may have even made a formal statement about what he or she believes is the issue. The researcher's role is to make sure that management has clearly and correctly stated the problem, opportunity, or question. To do so, the researcher will review the situation facing the decision maker and probably will conduct a situation analysis (see Chapter 3). It is important for the researcher and the decision maker to agree on the definition of the problem.

Step 2: Define the Research Objective and Information Needs

Once the researcher and the decision maker have agreed on the decision problem, the question of *what we want to know* needs to be addressed. Remember that the research is conducted to assist the decision maker with a specific issue. The underlying goal of this step is to identify the information that the decision maker needs to solve his or her problem. Very often the decision maker will have a sense of what he or she wants to know and will be able to identify a few research questions. For example, a marketing manager of a local hospital wants to know how effective his advertising campaign is. This research question could then be transformed into a research objective:

1. To determine the level of aided and unaided awareness, among the target audience, of the hospital and the services that are provided

The next task in this stage would be to define the specific information that will be needed to measure awareness (see Chapter 4).

Step 3: Select a Research Design

The research design stage of the research process includes a number of decisions that lay out the approach that will be taken during the research project. The research design is the plan that describes the methods and procedures that will be used to collect and analyze the data. The research design is a function of the research objectives and includes a determination of the type of data that will be collected, the data sources, and the data collection methodology. Most research objectives can be met by using one of three research designs: exploratory, descriptive, and causal.

The sources of data will be classified as either secondary or primary data (see Chapter 6). *Secondary data* are data that previously have been collected for some reason other than the current situation. *Primary data* are data that have been collected specifically for a current research problem or opportunity.

The research design also includes a determination regarding the data collection method. There are two fundamental ways to collect primary data. One is to ask questions, and the other is to observe behavior. Telephone interviews, self-administered surveys, online surveys, personal interviews, and focus groups are some of the methods used to ask questions. Observation methods might include trained human observers or a variety of mechanical devices such as video cameras, scanners, or tape recorders to record behaviors or events.

Step 4: Design the Research Instrument

When a research design calls for primary data to be collected, a data collection instrument must be designed to record the information. The questionnaire needs to produce information that is accurate and addresses the information needs that have been determined (see Chapter 7).

Step 5: Determine the Sample Plan

Designing a sampling plan requires that the researcher specify (1) the population of interest, (2) the sampling frame, which is the list of population elements from which the sample will be drawn, (3) the sample selection process, and (4) the sample size (see Chapter 8).

Step 6: Collect and Process the Data

Once the sample has been determined, data collection can begin. Once the data have been collected, several procedural activities must be performed before the data can be analyzed. The data have to be coded so that they can be entered into computer files and then cleaned of either data-entry or coding errors (see Chapter 9).

Step 7: Analyze and Interpret the Data

In this step, the researcher begins the process of turning raw data into useful information for the decision maker. Data analysis can vary widely in sophistication, from simple frequency distributions to descriptive measures (mean, median, mode, standard deviation) to more complex multivariate techniques (see Chapter 10).

Step 8: Present Research Findings to Decision Makers

The final research report needs to be presented to the decision makers. In some cases this report may be written; at other times it may consist of a PowerPoint presentation. Often the presentation will include both (see Chapter 11).

It should be clear that this project is going to require a commitment of time and effort beyond that normally associated with a pure "lecture" class. While the scope of the assignment may be intimidating at first, you will find the project to be a manageable and very interesting academic experience. *Good luck!*

Forming Your Group

Perhaps the most difficult problem you'll face with the project is one of management. You'll need to manage your team, your fellow team members, and yourself. Time management, priority setting, and attention to detail will be crucial throughout the project. If you are allowed to form your own group, choosing the individuals to work with may be one of the more important decisions you will make in the course. When thinking about potential group members consider a few of the following issues:

- *Schedules.* You'll need to find a regular time to meet throughout the semester. If someone works off campus during the time when you are available, scheduling problems are sure to develop. While you may be able to make effective use of the Internet and conduct some "virtual meetings," you probably will need to meet at least once a week. Be sure to agree to a few alternative times that will work for everyone.

- *Objectives.* This is a tough one to judge but is worth the effort. A student who is motivated and willing to do the work necessary to earn an A is going to have a difficult time working with someone who is happy to get out of the course with a C. During the first week of the semester, try to get a feel for this by observing your classmates.

- *Personal compatibility.* Again, this is a tough factor to judge. You are more likely to get the work accomplished if you get along than if you don't.

Team Charter

Early on (the second or third meeting) the group should establish a set of understandings (charter) with regard to how you plan to operate. For example, what will be your policy on group meetings? How often should you meet and for how long, and what happens when someone misses a meeting? Likewise, how will the group make decisions: consensus or majority? How will the team deal with members who don't participate or contribute in a way that meets the agreed upon norms? How should meetings be conducted, formally with minutes taken or informally? These are just a few of the issues you will need to address. A good way to handle this before problems arise is to develop an agreement that sets out agreed upon group policies on these and other issues and is then signed by each member of the group. A good format for this agreement is presented below:

1. *Schedule of meetings.* Describe the frequency of meetings, the times at which meetings generally will be held, and the location of the meetings

2. *Attendance policy.* Describe expectations with regard to attendance at team meetings and the procedure to follow if a member must miss a meeting.

3. *Participation expectations.* Describe expectations with regard to participation and processes designed to encourage equal participation. Discuss a procedure to deal with a member who is not meeting expectations.

4. *Decision making.* How will decisions be made: by consensus, majority vote, and so on?

5. *Sanctions.* If someone fails to meet performance expectations, describe the procedures that will be used to address the issue. Addressing this issue in the charter gives

each member a clear understanding of the process that will be used and keeps the problem from becoming personal. Some groups have used the following:

a. Verbal warning
b. Written warning
c. Poor evaluation
d. Termination from the group

6. *Signatures.* Each member should sign the document, indicating his or her agreement and willingness to participate within the agreed upon framework.

Spending a little time at the beginning of the process is sure to save you time in the long run and result in a more enjoyable and productive experience. One of the most difficult tasks you will face with a group project is getting the entire group together on a regular basis to review progress and plan for the next step. You should establish a regular weekly meeting time as well as one or two alternative meeting times. You should also explore ways to utilize the Internet to share information between meetings. You may decide that each written phase to be discussed at a group meeting should be disseminated at least 24 hours before the scheduled meeting. Utilizing the Internet in this way will improve the quality of your work and probably shorten your meeting times.

Team Evaluation

At the end of the semester you will be asked to evaluate the contributions of the members in your group. Your instructor will provide you with a form, or you may use the form contained in Appendix 1B. The form requests that you evaluate only the other members of your group. However, you may use the comments section to point out various aspects of your contribution to the group. The instructor will assign an overall grade to the group project and give separate grades to each individual member. Some team members may benefit from their extra hard work, and others may be penalized for failing to meet expectations. The instructor may utilize the grading rubric provided in Appendix 1C or a separate rubric. In either case, it will be useful to pay careful attention to the requirements at each stage of the process.

Marketing Research: Peer Evaluation

Project _____

Semester _____

For each member in your group, evaluate the quality of contribution throughout the semester. Consider the individual's contribution in terms of the following scale:

Grade

9–10 The individual who earns this evaluation has consistently contributed. He or she has demonstrated an understanding of the material, a willingness to work consistently to achieve a high-quality product, to help others, and to be flexible in scheduling. Essentially this assessment indicates that the individual has done more than his or her "fair share" and has shown initiative and interest throughout the semester. If everyone in the group worked at this level, the project would have been a definite A.

7–8 An individual who earns this evaluation has contributed in an average way. Performance was generally good but perhaps was inconsistent. This individual did the tasks that were assigned to him or her but rarely took the initiative. Inconsistent attendance at meetings or lack of preparation at times that slowed your progress or other similar tendencies at times diminished a generally solid contribution. This individual usually contributed his or her fair share, and if everyone in the group worked at this level, the project would have been graded somewhere in the C+ to B+ range.

5–6 This evaluation indicates that the individual performed below reasonable expectations. Whether it was quality of work, attendance at meetings, preparation, interest in the project, initiative, understanding of the material, or meeting deadlines, this individual performed at a level below what one would expect. Essentially, the group would have been better off without the contributions of this person. If everyone in the group performed at this level, the project would probably receive a D if it were completed on time.

1–4 This range indicates that the individual made insignificant contributions, if any, to the project and was essentially dead weight. This individual made a minimal effort to get involved and basically depended on others to do the work. This person barely deserves to have his or her name on the project, though he or she may have contributed at some point during the semester. If everyone performed at this level, the project probably wouldn't have been completed.

Evaluating a peer is a difficult thing to do whether it's in a class or on the job. However, for a team project like the one in this course to work and for the workload to be fairly distributed, everyone needs to contribute. A student who has contributed significantly should be recognized with an assessment that reflects that contribution. Likewise, a student who did not meet expectations should not benefit from the work of others. In the space below, provide an evaluation of each member of the team. You should use the evaluation criteria described above to assign a numeric evaluation. Feel free to write a brief explanation of your assessment for each team member

Name _____ *Evaluation* _____

_____

_____

_____

_____

_____

Comments:

Score Sheet: Marketing Research Project

Student Names _____

_____

Project Name _____ Semester _____

1. *Review of Decision Situation*   10 points
Has adequate background been provided on the company, competition, and industry to put the situation faced by the decision makers in the proper perspective? Has the rationale for this research project been clearly explained, and its contribution to decision making described? Have the objectives been clearly specified?

Comments: _____

_____

_____

2. *Review of Research Objectives and Information Needs*   10 points
Have the research objectives been clearly stated? Do they relate to decision objectives? Have the information needs been listed? Are they relevant yet comprehensive?

Comments: _____

_____

_____

3. *Review of Literature*   15 points
Has the information obtained through the literature review been evaluated as to relevance, quality, and timeliness? Has the information been summarized and reported clearly? Have multiple sources been utilized appropriately? Do the results provide greater insight into the research problem? Have all sources been cited appropriately? This section should focus on a review of literature that includes concept definition, methodologies used, and measurements employed in cited studies.

Comments: _____

_____

_____

4. *Research Design*   10 points
Has the concept been clearly defined, and the *process* used to identify the core factors or dimensions of the concept been described? What research design was used (exploratory, descriptive, causal)? What were the secondary sources of data that were used? What were the procedures used to collect primary data (observation or questioning), and what was the method of contact (mail, online, telephone, personal)? Has a methodology for data collection that is appropriate been chosen and justified?

Comments: _____
_____
_____
_____

5. *Sampling Plan*   15 points
    a. *Definition of the Population*   4 points
        Has the population been properly defined in terms of elements, sampling units, extent, and time?
    b. *Sampling Frame*   2 points
        Has a sampling frame been identified that is available and proper considering the population?
    c. *Sample Size*   5 points
        Has the sample size been arrived at by an acceptable procedure? Is it appropriate considering time, cost, and desired precision?
    d. *Sampling Procedures*   4 points
        Has a sampling procedure been selected and justified relative to alternative procedures?
    Comments: _____
    _____
    _____

6. *Questionnaire*   15 points
    Does the questionnaire cover the necessary information that was listed in the information needs section? Is the wording simple yet clear? Does the questionnaire avoid leading or biasing questions? Are the questions properly sequenced? Have the questions anticipated the ability of the respondent to respond accurately? Does the questionnaire contain clear instructions and have an attractive layout?
    Comments: _____
    _____

7. *Data Analysis Strategy*   10 points
    Do mock-up tables clearly show the analysis that will be utilized? Does this analysis provide the information that is necessary to reach a decision?
    Comments: _____
    _____
    _____

8. *Proposed Schedule*   5 points
    Does the schedule clearly identify the dates and length of time for each stage of the research process?
    Comments: _____
    _____
    _____

9. *Paper*   10 points
    While the written proposal contains the entire output of the project and is reflected in all the previous categories, this section is meant to specifically review the content and means of presentation of the written materials with regard to spelling, sentence structure, bibliography, and so on.
    Comments: _____
    _____
    _____

CHAPTER 2

Choosing a Topic

Introduction

Your first assignment will involve the selection and submission of one or more project ideas. Your instructor will help you choose the most appropriate study for the purposes of the assignment. There are a number of ways research may be applied to assist marketing decision making, and many different studies provide valuable insights into key issues of concern for marketing managers. Many of these studies may not be appropriate for the purposes of this project assignment because they would require a greater level of expertise than a beginning researcher possesses. Others may not fit because they may involve only some of the skills that this project is designed to address. Your professor will be able to help you select the most appropriate study for this project.

This manual is designed to guide you through the various steps of a marketing research project. This manual is oriented toward the performance of a customer satisfaction study, a market segmentation study, an attitude and usage study, or a product concept study. Certainly there are a number of other types of research study that could be conducted; however, these studies have proved to be useful and doable and give students a wide range of exposure to marketing research issues that will be applicable to other types of research studies.

A quick look at the nature of the various studies may help you as you consider several project alternatives.

Customer Satisfaction Studies

Customer satisfaction results from a comparison between the level of service that a customer expects and the level of service that has been delivered. When service falls below expectations, customer dissatisfaction is likely to result. Since most consumption experiences are based on a number of factors, customer satisfaction studies generally provide considerable detail regarding a wide range of service attributes. For example, satisfaction with a retail clothing store may be based on a number of factors, such as merchandise assortment, quality, price, and service. A customer satisfaction study will need to identify those relevant attributes in order to capture the customer's attitude fully.

The measurement of customer satisfaction is a rapidly growing area of marketing research and is a key aspect of a firm's efforts at customer relationship management. There is a strong correlation between customer satisfaction and customer retention. Some recent studies have indicated that 95 percent of customers who rate service as "excellent" will repurchase from an organization and are "highly unlikely" to switch to another product or service provider. Other studies have shown that although customers tend to be dissatisfied with up to 25 percent of their purchases, they are unlikely to complain. Most dissatisfied customers will buy less or switch suppliers. Responsive companies attempt to measure satisfaction regularly and to put in place measures designed to improve performance and increase satisfaction. These measures are designed to increase customer retention and help the company benefit from the high lifetime value a customer represents.

Customer satisfaction studies are usually conducted only among the firm's own customers. Organizations, large and small, have come to realize that it is more cost-effective to focus their efforts on retaining existing customers than to attempt to attract new customers.

Customer satisfaction studies provide management with a monitoring tool that allows them to correct perceived problems before they result in large losses in the customer base. Customer satisfaction surveys are an important tool in a firm's *customer relationship management (CRM)* efforts.

Market Segmentation Studies

You may have first heard the term *market segmentation* in your marketing principles class. However, you have observed the segmentation of markets since you were very young. The soft drink market is a good example of a market that has been segmented. From Diet Coke to caffeine-free flavored colas to noncolas, the industry has attempted to identify and serve diverse segments. Firms utilizing a segmentation strategy seek to group potential customers into homogeneous groups that are large enough to be profitably served, are accessible, and behave similarly in response to marketing stimuli.

A *market segment* consists of a group of customers who share a similar set of wants and respond to marketing stimuli in a similar manner. Segmentation involves dividing the market of potential customers into homogeneous subgroups. These subgroups may be distinguished in terms of their behavior patterns, demographic characteristics, attitudes and lifestyles, and geographic location. Segmentation is used frequently when a brand lacks the resources required to compete successfully and to differentiate itself from the competition in the mass market. A company may benefit in many ways from an effective segmentation strategy. The company can create a product that is closer to the ideal point of its customers and can price it appropriately, communicate its benefits more efficiently, and distribute it more appropriately than a mass marketing strategy would allow. *Market segmentation* is the first step in *target marketing,* which is the decision regarding how many and which segments to target. These distinct groups may require separate product or marketing mixes. There are a number of ways to segment a market, but a useful segmentation study identifies a well-defined market segment that probably will respond in a similar way to a given set of marketing stimuli.

Market segmentation studies are common among businesses and are used to improve their marketing efforts. Segmentation studies group customers into segments based on similar needs and benefits sought and then estimate the size and characteristics of the segments, the media habits of segment members, and the likely response to different marketing mix elements and programs.

Consumer markets may be segmented by looking at consumer geographic, demographic, behavioral, and psychographic characteristics, examining whether the potential segments exhibit different responses to marketing mix elements. Consumer responses regarding benefits, use occasions, and usage rate may also be used to segments markets.

Too often marketing managers will talk about the female market or the elderly market, ignoring the obvious—that within those large and increasingly important markets, there are significant differences that distinguish women or the elderly. A segmentation study that explores ways to segment one of these or other diverse markets would fit the project goals very nicely.

Concept Testing

New product development is critical for most companies to remain competitive. An essential step in new product development is the initial evaluation of new product ideas, called *concept testing*. Concept testing is part of the prescreening stage of the process of new product development. It occurs before management begins the expensive work of technical development. The concept test is designed to identify promising new ideas for further development and identify poor concepts so that they may be eliminated. Concept tests also provide a rough estimate of the sales rate that could be anticipated for the new product by asking potential buyers to state their intention to purchase the new product. While the value of these estimates is controversial, a measure of buying intention appears in most concept tests. Companies use the results to assess the viability of the new product before making major resource commitments for its development.

A *new product concept* is a statement about product features that will provide selected benefits compared to other products or solutions. Preparation of a concept statement is the first step in concept testing. A concept statement states the new product's differences compared to existing alternatives. The concept statement should be a short, clear statement that provides a description of the key attributes that may affect the buying decision, relating the benefits to the consumer in a way that is credible and relevant. Often the concept statement will be supplemented by a product drawing or diagram, and occasionally a more expensive prototype will be developed to provide a clearer understanding of the proposed product. Respondents are then asked to state their intentions to purchase when the product becomes available.

One of the most popular purchase intention measures is a five-point scale similar to the following: *Considering the new product description you just read, please indicate your intention to buy it when it becomes available*:

- Definitely will buy it
- Probably will buy it
- Might or might not buy it
- Probably will not buy it
- Definitely will not buy it

Concept testing has its limitations and doesn't work particularly well in situations where (1) the prime benefit is sensual, such as the taste of a new food or the aroma of a perfume, (2) the new product utilizes new technology that the consumer cannot visualize, or (3) the new product addresses a problem that consumers may not readily identify with.

For fuller coverage of the new product development process and the role of concept testing, as well as methodological issues associated with concept testing, consult a standard text such as *New Products Development*, seventh edition, by C. Merle Crawford and C. Anthony Di Benedetto (McGraw-Hill).

Customer Attitudes and Usage Studies

The importance of understanding the customer has long been an accepted axiom in marketing. An understanding of attitudes is useful in understanding consumers' and industrial buyers' marketplace behaviors. Whether the decision involves product design, pricing, promotion, or any number of marketing stimuli, marketing managers look to understand and positively influence customers' attitudes, beliefs, and perceptions and how customers' product usage varies within and across market segments.

Understanding the customer—how the customer makes the purchase decision and why—is critical input to most marketing management decisions. Efforts are under way that utilize such diverse disciplines as neuroscience, linguistics, psychology, and anthropology to learn how customers think. New techniques such as neuromarketing, which uses brain scans to provide images of brain activity at crucial moments of product choice, are being tested. While new technologies offer the promise of a better understanding of how customers think, marketers continue to be interested in psychological factors that affect customers' actions toward their products and services and marketing researchers regularly measure these factors as a way to understand why customers buy and how customers think. Although measuring consumer attitudes is a difficult process with relatively imprecise scales, marketing researchers continue to attach significant importance to the identification of attitudes as a way to diagnose strengths and weaknesses in the marketplace.

For our purposes, an *attitude* is defined as a learned tendency to perceive and act in a consistently favorable or unfavorable manner with regard to a given object or idea. Attitude is an important concept in marketing because it is believed to influence behavior strongly.

Attitude is believed by many marketers to directly affect purchase and usage experiences, which in turn directly affect future attitudes toward the product or service. Marketers' efforts to influence buying behavior, whether through changes in promotion, price, product, or place, often begin with key questions regarding customers' attitudes toward the product or service and their usage patterns.

While customer satisfaction, concept tests, and market segmentation studies are clearly focused as to the objectives of the study, a decision to conduct an attitude study will require careful attention to the link between the decision to be made and the research objectives. Attitude and usage studies could contribute to marketing decision making in a number of ways and are among the most frequently conducted marketing research activities. Make sure you have a clear understanding of the decision problem before you commit. Always ask, *"What would we need to know in order to make a decision in this situation?"*

The Client

Along with the selection of the type of project will be the selection of the client or "simulated client." If your class requires work with an actual client, you may be assigned to work with a local business, nonprofit organization, or campus group. If that is the case, the type of study you conduct will stem from the needs of the organization and will require a meeting with the client to ascertain the marketing problem to be addressed by the research. Other professors may ask you to determine the type of study you want to conduct and then find an appropriate local client. In that situation, you may decide to conduct a customer satisfaction study, for example, and then look for a client who is interested in your project. Since your study is likely to be offered to the client at little or no charge, you should be able to find a willing and enthusiastic client.

Once a client has been identified and you've had a chance to become familiar with the company through a review of secondary data, you'll want to meet with the client to refine the project scope and better define the research problem. Prior to the client meeting, you'll want to read as much as you can about the company, the industry, and the competition to be better prepared for the meeting. During the initial meeting the decision maker probably will describe the problem and the information that is needed. The objective of meeting with the client is to enable the researcher, working with the manager, to translate the decision problem into a research problem. At the initial meeting, you may want to explore with the decision maker the following general questions designed to ensure that the true decision problem will be addressed by the research:

- What were the events that led to the decision to conduct research?
- What actions are contemplated on the basis of the research?
- What alternatives are being considered in order to address the problem?
- What questions does the decision maker need to have answered in order to take a course of action?
- What criteria will the decision maker consider when deciding among the alternatives?
- What is the customer base from which the information should be collected?
- What is the time frame for a decision?

Additionally you will want to explore key issues associated with the company's marketing efforts:

- What factors does the manager believe drive consumer behavior? Is it price, product quality, product features, and so on?
- Who is the major competition?
- How are the firm's prices compared to those of the competition?

- What are the key elements of the firm's promotional efforts?
- How does the firm define its trading area?
- How does the firm attempt to differentiate itself from the competition?

Consider these questions as the starting point as you prepare for the client meeting and remember that the degree of client cooperation you can expect will be dependent on the client's perception of your professionalism. In addition to your ability to ask appropriate questions, the client's perceptions will be affected by your attire and behavior at the meeting.

If your assignment calls for you to work with a "simulated client," you will need to select a study type and then review the business press for an organization that would be likely to utilize such a study. Often projects with simulated clients are required at schools in areas that are relatively isolated from the surrounding community. Working with a simulated client will mean that you will need to gather a great deal of information about the client and its industry, utilizing secondary data.

The Assignment

Your first assignment is to submit one or more project ideas on the designated date. Consider ideas that are of interest to members of the group and identify the potential client for each idea. The following is a small sample of the projects that have been conducted by students in the author's classes during a recent semester:

- A study to measure student satisfaction with the campus dining halls
- A study to measure alumni satisfaction with the School of Business
- A descriptive study of listeners of the local public radio station
- A study of student perceptions of the services offered and quality of care at the local hospital
- A concept test of a new privately funded student housing development in the college vicinity
- An attitude and behavior study of students' use of fitness centers on campus
- An analysis of attitudes of shoppers within the trade area for "downtown merchants"

The Group Meeting

All the members of the group should come to this meeting with at least two ideas for a project that has the potential to maintain their interest for a full semester. Think about companies that you may want to work for in the future or firms that you currently work for; consider campus organizations or services that you are involved in or utilize. After some discussion, the group should be able reach consensus on a few ideas. The instructor should be able to help you fine-tune these ideas into a doable semester project.

What to Submit

The project topic that is submitted should be typed, contain the names of each group member, and include the type of study and the hypothetical client.

List three alternative project ideas. (Be as specific as you can.)

1. _____

2. _____

3. _____

For each alternative, consider the following:

Interest. Does this alternative excite you? Is this something you would like to learn more about?

Time. Does this alternative require a methodology that may not fit into the time schedule available to you this semester?

Skills. Are the skills that will be required within the scope of the course in terms of methodological and statistical skills?

Complexity. Does this project alternative require knowledge of advanced methods or marketing techniques that may be beyond the scope of your current level of preparation?

CHAPTER 3

Review of the Decision Situation

Introduction

The fundamental purpose of marketing research is to provide useful information that allows marketing decision makers to be better informed and more likely to make decisions that produce superior results. A marketing manager may bring years of experience and a managerial instinct to the decision-making process yet still feel the need for additional information. At the same time, a marketing researcher brings a set of skills that promotes a structured, step-by-step approach to gathering and analyzing information that will aid in decision making. However, for the researcher to add value and provide useful information, he or she needs to understand the situation facing the marketing manager.

Decision Situation

A marketing manager's job is difficult because of the continuous changes in the competitive situation that must be considered and anticipated. The marketplace is changing swiftly and radically as a result of major forces such as globalization, technological advances such as the Internet that have fostered greater connectivity between customers and companies, and behavioral changes among customers who expect higher quality and service and are at the same time increasingly price-sensitive.

The marketing manager faces an uncertain environment and is called upon to make a number of strategic and tactical decisions that require quality information. Among the decisions a marketing manager may be considering could be the following:

Planning
- What market segments provide the greatest opportunity?
- What customers should we target?
- How should we position the brand?

Problem solving
- What brand identity should we be trying to build?
- What packaging should we use?
- What price should we charge?
- What role should price have in promoting our product?
- Where and by whom should we sell our products?
- How much should we spend on advertising? What should the allocation for each brand be?
- What media mix should we employ?

Control
- How satisfied with our offerings are our customers?
- What customers are we losing and why?
- What is our overall market share?
- What is our image with the trade? With our customers? With our suppliers?
- What is the level of awareness of our brand among our target customers?

These are only a few of the many decisions and questions a marketing manager may be facing that call for additional input from the marketing research function. The decision maker has the initial responsibility for determining that a decision problem exists that might benefit from the services of a researcher. Once the researcher is brought into the situation, he or she needs to develop a complete understanding of the problem facing the decision maker. The researcher will question the decision maker as described in Chapter 2 in order to develop insights into how the decision maker perceives the problem. With a basic understanding of why the research is needed, the researcher needs to focus on the circumstances surrounding the problem. For research to provide credible assistance to the marketing manager, an understanding of the situation facing the decision maker is critical. It is in this context that this stage of the project falls. Your task is to familiarize yourself with the situation facing the marketing manager in a way that enhances your ability to provide relevant information.

The Assignment

The second assignment for this project requires you to conduct a brief situation analysis that details your understanding of the situation facing the marketing manager for your "client" firm. Every outside researcher needs to "get up to speed" quickly when dealing with a new client in order to understand the client and the situation facing the client. The analysis should include the components presented below and should be presented in a way that gives your instructor insight into the management problem that your research will be addressing.

This section should conclude with a summary that synthesizes what your analysis has revealed. As you prepare this section of your project, keep in mind the purpose of this analysis: It is to provide the researcher with the necessary background information that should provide insights into the situation confronting the marketing manager. For a researcher to provide value, to offer new insights into a situation, the researcher must familiarize himself or herself with what is known that is relevant to the situation and, perhaps more important, what is not known.

Situation Analysis

A situation analysis is a tool that focuses on the informal gathering of background information that sheds light on the events and factors that have led to the current situation. It is your responsibility as the researcher for this project to develop your understanding of the client's business. To do this, you must go beyond the information provided by the client, gathering information from trade publications, government documents, and other secondary sources that provide an objective understanding of the client's business. Don't rely on information provided solely by the client, because in your role as an outside consultant you are expected to add to the information base rather than recycle it. You'll want to understand the client's situation, which includes an examination of the industry, the competition, the customers, and the company itself.

The eternal triangle in marketing analysis, the 3 C's of marketing, includes an analysis of the company, the customer, and the competition.

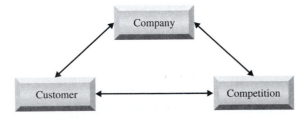

Relevant information is information that relates to the situation faced by the marketing manager. Discuss the situation facing the manager but do not include an exhaustive historical review. Describing the firm's history from the founding of the company in the 1800s to the present may make sense on the company Web site but isn't appropriate in this section of your report. Identifying relevant information is difficult for the practicing manager and for the marketing researcher. There is frequently an overabundance of facts and figures.

Determining what matters and what doesn't is a skill that is best developed through experience. This phase of the project will require that you begin to develop that skill.

The framework that follows is a useful way to organize your analysis. Keep in mind as you prepare this section that the end result should be an understanding of the factors that drive the need for information. If you were conducting a customer satisfaction study, for example, an in-depth analysis of the customer and the factors that drive satisfaction would be critical. At the same time, it would be essential that the researcher become familiar with the firm's claims regarding the product and the accompanying service as well as those of the competition. In the sections below, suggested areas for analysis are provided.

Company Analysis

Take a look at the situation the company is in. The following questions should go a long way toward providing the insights needed to understand the company.

- Is it a small, locally owned and operated business or a large multinational?
- What are the firm's strengths and weaknesses?
- Is it a market leader, a close second, or a distant follower?
- Is it considered innovative or a "me-too" kind of firm?
- What are the relevant trends for this product or service?
- How well has the product or service been performing in the recent past?
- What are the measures of performance that the firm uses?
- Is it a single-product or single-service firm, or does it have a number of products or services in the product mix?
- How important is this particular product or service to the organization?
- Is the firm known to offer superior products? Does it have significant marketing strengths such as a known brand name, a great reputation, or an outstanding distribution system?
- What are the primary product claims that it promotes?

While not all of these questions will apply in all situations, they do provide a good starting point for an outside researcher to become familiar with the company.

Customer Analysis

This section should provide some basic insights into the customer.

- Who are the customers? Check out an appropriate volume of *Simmons Study of Media and Markets* if your library subscribes to it. You'll find a great deal of demographic information as well as information about media usage.
- Are the primary customers also the primary users?
- What is the customer really buying; that is, what benefits is the customer looking to fulfill?
- What factors drive consumption, and what factors are most responsible for customer satisfaction or dissatisfaction?
- What market segments does the firm target, and what are the characteristics of the particular segments served by this product or service? You might describe a particular market segment by using standard descriptor variables that fall into four major categories:
  - *Geographic.* The underlying rationale is that tastes vary by part of the world, part of a country, or even between cities and rural areas.
  - *Demographic.* Income, age, occupation, education, race, gender, and other variables have been found to influence consumers' buying habits.

- *Psychographic.* This refers to the psychological differences between people in terms of lifestyles, personalities, and social class.
- *Behavioral.* Occasions, benefits, user status, usage rate, and loyalty status are thought by many marketers to be the starting point for constructing market segments.
- How large is the market, and is it growing rapidly, slowly, or not at all?

Competitor Analysis

Once a company has identified its primary competitors, it needs to understand some basic characteristics of the major competitors. Specifically, an understanding of the marketing strategies, the marketing objectives, and the strengths and weaknesses of each major competitor is needed to more fully understand the decision situation facing the client. An assessment of current marketing strategies would include the segments pursued, how the firm is positioning the products or services, and an evaluation of the firm's price and quality strategies.

Specific questions that should be considered follow:

- What are the key industry trends that affect this situation?
- Who are the major competitors?
- What are their strengths and weaknesses, strategies, sizes, and market shares?
- What trends will affect future competition?
- What trends will affect substitutes for the company's products?
- What are the primary product claims of each major competitor?
- Is the firm known to have significant marketing strengths in terms of distribution, brand image, quality, and so on?
- How is each competitor positioned in terms of price and quality?

By providing a structured analysis of the decision situation confronting marketing management, you should have a pretty good understanding of the success factors in this particular market. You will also be able to provide a context for the study. Why is it being done, and how would management benefit from this study?

Once you understand the decision situation, you should be in a better position to work with the decision maker to define the decision problem more properly, distinguishing symptoms from the root problem.

Sources

You'll need to use a variety of sources for this phase of the project. Business publications such as *BusinessWeek, Advertising Age,* and the *Wall Street Journal* (www.wsj.com) should help. Check out www.bizjournals.com to search over 40 local business weeklies. You may need to examine trade publications that are specific to the particular industry or take a look at trade associations (search Google for "trade associations"). Utilize the databases available to you through your library. The following should be very helpful:

- ABI/INFORM Trade & Industry
- LexisNexis Academic
- Business and Company Resource Center with Investext Plus

This section of the paper should be roughly two to four pages and should provide insight into the company and the decision situation it faces.

CHAPTER 4

Research Objectives and Information Needs

Introduction

One of the most valuable contributions of marketing research is related to its role in the problem definition stage of marketing decision making. Only when a problem is properly identified can pertinent information be provided. Part of the process of problem formulation requires the identification of research objectives. This section of your project involves the identification of research objectives and subsequently the breakdown of those objectives into information needs.

Decision Situation

Your research project begins with the recognition that its ultimate value is based on the extent to which it provides decision makers with information that enhances their ability to solve marketing problems and exploit marketing opportunities. Let's assume that the decision makers for your client are facing a situation in which past experiences, assumptions, and so on, are not considered sufficient and that they have decided that additional information is required. The research process has been activated by the decision makers' recognition of a marketing decision problem or opportunity situation or a need to monitor performance. Your task is to provide information that will be used and useful even as you recognize that a great deal of marketing research goes unused. Considering the decision situation and the associated information requirements is critical to the successful completion of your project.

While the research process is generally described in the context of management decision making, it should be pointed out that many marketing research projects tend to be discovery-oriented and are really first steps in a process that provides the decision maker with greater insights into and understanding of the customer or competitive environment. Once the research process has been initiated, it is important to the ultimate success of your project that you identify the nature of the decision situation and provide information that is relevant to the decision maker.

Most textbooks use the term *decision problem* in the broadest sense to refer to situations in which management faces marketing *problems* that involve a great deal of uncertainty as well as to situations that represent significant *opportunities*. In both cases, uncertainty as to which course of action offers the greatest probability of meeting a specified marketing objective requires information that reduces that level of uncertainty. For your research to be useful, then, it needs to recognize the alternatives and provide management with information that enhances its ability to decide among them. Understanding the criteria that will be utilized to choose among the alternatives gives the researcher an appropriate basis to determine the relevance of potential information to the decision maker.

There should be a clear understanding between the researcher and the decision maker as to the nature of the decision situation and the role marketing research is expected to play in the decision process. Once the decision maker's need for information has been determined, a formal statement that describes the decision situation should be written down and formally agreed upon by the researcher and the decision maker. In the last chapter you learned how to conduct an analysis of the decision situation. Armed with a formal analysis, which should be endorsed by the client to produce additional clarity and prevent later misunderstandings, it is now time to reframe the decision problems into research problems.

Decision Problem to Research Objectives

Simply put, *research objectives* specify what you want to know when the project has been completed. They are stated in terms of knowledge to be gained and are derived from the decision problem. *Decision objectives* identify the managerial objectives for the decision that is being considered and generally are stated in managerially relevant metrics (e.g., increase sales by 8 percent in the first quarter). To add value to the decision-making process, the researcher needs to identify what the marketing manager needs to know in order to make a decision that will allow him or her to reach the stated decision objective. The decision maker's objectives are rarely stated explicitly to the researcher, or they may not be stated accurately or precisely. For example, the marketing manager might state that the firm wants customers to perceive the brand as the "best in the market" without elaborating on that characterization. The researcher must transform terms such as *high quality* and *market leader* into specific, operational objectives that the research can serve. One means of doing that consists of engaging the decision maker in a discussion regarding potential solutions to the problem to see whether the decision maker would follow a given course of action. Often such a conversation will reveal the "real objectives."

With a detailed understanding of the decision situation, you will need to translate the decision problem into information terms that will guide the development of your project. A few examples may illustrate the distinctions between the decision problem and the research problem. Suppose a marketing manager who is looking to increase sales is considering a brand extension decision. The great uncertainty may rest with the market segment that should be targeted. If the manager *knew* which segment offered the greatest potential for this brand, he or she would increase the chances of meeting the decision objectives. Thus, the *decision objective* of increasing sales by 8 percent would translate to a *research objective* of "identifying the market potential for each of the identified market segments." The decision problem involves what needs to be done. The research problem involves determining what information is needed to decide among the alternatives that the decision maker may be considering. Redefining the decision problem in information terms is a crucial step in the research process.

Another example may help illustrate the importance of this phase of the research process. Suppose a group of "downtown" merchants in a small community became alarmed at the decrease they were noticing in store traffic in their stores and wanted to know what they should do about it. There could be many reasons for the decrease in traffic, including a change in the retail store mix in the downtown shopping district, changes in the demographic composition of the trade area, increased competition from neighboring communities, and ineffective advertising. For the merchants to develop a plan to increase store traffic, they recognize the need to understand whatever changes in image that consumers may have of shopping in the downtown area. Thus, their desire to increase store traffic translates into a research problem that calls for the assessment of image of the shopping district. In another example, a general manager for a new car dealer has observed a decline in sales at his dealership even as sales nationwide are increasing. Of course the manager wants to reverse the decline, but he is not sure what has caused it. After a thorough review of the local competitive and economic environment using exploratory research indicates that the problem probably rests within the dealership, the research problem is defined as the evaluation of customer satisfaction.

The main way to avoid researching the wrong decision problem is to develop a proper understanding of the decision situation (see Chapter 3). If the decision maker does not know what he or she wants to achieve, the research study will not fulfill its proper

EXHIBIT 4.1

Relationship between
Decision Situation
and Information
Requirements

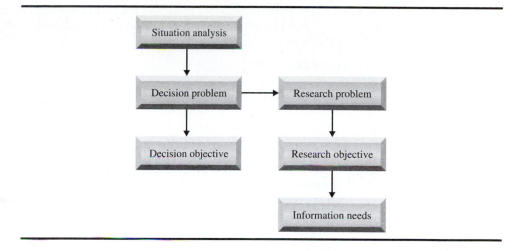

role. At the conclusion of the project, the researcher does not want to hear the dreaded words "That's interesting, but it doesn't help me very much." If you are working with a client, and even if you're not, you would be well advised to draft a statement that describes your understanding of the problem. The statement should include the following items:

- *The initial events* that led to a need for the decision to act. These events may help the researcher better understand the nature of the research problem.
- *The actions* that are being considered to address the problem.
- *The information* that the decision maker needs to decide on a course of action.
- *An explanation of how each piece of the information* will be used to help make the decision.

The linkage between the situation facing the decision maker and the information that will ultimately be gathered is described above and illustrated in Exhibit 4.1.

Appropriate research objectives might take a form similar to the following:

- Determine the level of customer satisfaction among shoppers at the college bookstore during the fall semester.
- Measure satisfaction with regard to academic programs among alumni of the School of Business who have graduated within the past five years.

Note that in addition to specifying what you *want to know,* the objective also identifies the *relevant group* to be studied and the *appropriate time period.*

Information Needs

Information needs are a detailed breakdown of the research objectives. In Chapter 5 of this manual, we will examine the determinants of customer satisfaction for a new automobile. Using the results of our literature review, where we have identified the determinants of customer satisfaction, we have listed these determinants as part of the information needs. Let's preview the example in the next chapter relating to satisfaction with an automobile.

The determinants of customer satisfaction for a new automobile listed in Chapter 5 are

- Mechanical quality
- Feature and accessory quality
- Performance
- Comfort
- Style

The information needs portion of the project will require that you break down each of these items to specific items that will need to be assessed. Let's consider comfort. A quick examination of that dimension will suggest that the following items fall under the category:

- COMFORT
  - Headroom
  - Legroom
  - Seats
  - Temperature controls

Likewise, you would want to identify the components of each of the determinants identified. You'll need to get very specific here and should consult product brochures, product reviews, and so forth, to help you identify the relevant components. Taken together, these components would be specified and listed as the information needs. It is likely that you will have multiple items for each determinant of customer satisfaction.

This is a critical section of your proposal because it will determine the information that you attempt to gather. The results of this section will be utilized as you put your questionnaire together. In fact, once the research objectives and information needs have been identified, the design of the questionnaire will involve largely decisions regarding question wording, format, and layout. What you need to ask will have been determined in this phase of the research project.

While you will need to clearly identify your research objectives and then the information needs based on the decision situation, consider that most studies also need to include a breakdown of the results utilizing demographic factors. For example, you may want to know if there is a difference between satisfied and dissatisfied consumers based on gender, age, or income. *You'll need to identify the classification factors you will be looking at in this section as well.*

The Assignment

The research objectives and information needs section is probably the most important part of your research project. The assignment for this section of your project flows from the analysis of the decision situation and requires that you identify the list of research objectives with corresponding information needs that will focus on information that will help the decision maker make better marketing decisions. It is important to state clearly the need for information in decision terms and link the research objectives to the decision situation.

Below are some common research objectives that should be illustrative:

- To measure customer satisfaction with the brand or service
- To determine consumer awareness of the brand
- To determine customers' attitudes regarding differentiating characteristics among brands within the category
- To measure the importance customers place on various product attributes
- To determine the relative sizes of alternative market segments
- To measure the relevant demographic characteristics of the target market

Information needs will then be a more detailed breakdown of the research objectives. The following examples may help illustrate the relationships further.

Situation   As part of an ongoing program designed to achieve the highest levels of customer satisfaction in the industry, Honda regularly monitors the satisfaction of new car buyers.

Decision Problem   Improve customer satisfaction of new car buyers to become the leader in the industry.

Research Objective   Measure levels of customer satisfaction among new Honda car buyers who have purchased within the last six months with regard to comfort, mechanical quality, performance, style, and feature and accessory quality.

Information Needs

1. *With regard to comfort,* measure the level of satisfaction with
   - Headroom
   - Legroom
   - Seats
   - Temperature controls
2. *With regard to mechanical quality,* measure the level of satisfaction with
   - Steering
   - Suspension
   - Brake system
   - Transmission

Another example may help illustrate the relationship between the decision situation, the research objectives, and information needs.

Situation   Suppose that the management of a small retail women's store that featured casual wear was concerned about decreases in store traffic and sales. Management was unclear about what the store image was among consumers in the primary trade area.

Decision Problem   Should the store's merchandise quality, prices, advertising, or service quality be modified, and do these factors affect store image?

Research Objective   Measure customers' attitudes toward the store in order to assess overall store image.

Information Needs   Measure customers' perceptions of

- Merchandise quality

- Merchandise assortment

- Store's return policy

- Sales associates

While this list of information needs is not exhaustive, it does illustrate the relationship between the situation analysis statement, the decision problem, the research objective, and information needs. Remember that the research objectives (or research questions) specify the information that is needed in the study and may be worded as either a statement or a question. The information needs represent a detailed listing of the items that, when taken together, make up the research objective.

You will find that the research objectives and information needs that you have identified for this stage of the project will represent the data requirements that will be the basis for the development of your data collection instrument.

CHAPTER 5

Literature Review

Introduction

You have been asked to design a research project for a real or simulated client and have been told that the project should be a customer satisfaction study, a market segmentation study, a customer attitude and usage study, a new product concept study, or some other type of study that your professor has suggested. Given that this is an introductory course in marketing research, it is probably fair to assume that you have little if any experience with these studies. The purpose of this phase of your project is quite simple: You want to learn how a typical marketing research study is conducted. In other words, there is no reason to reinvent the wheel (pardon the cliché). If there is a standard methodology, you should know that, and if there isn't, you should know that also.

This section isn't a standard part of a typical research proposal. A research agency typically has a history of completed projects for various clients that serve as testamony to its credibility and expertise. Since you are new to this, you can't claim extensive experience and in-depth knowledge of the issues associated with your particular type of study. For the purposes of this project, the literature review section is intended to serve as a summary of the current state of knowledge in the area of investigation, with special emphasis on the methodological issues associated with the particular study. When you have identified how others have conducted this type of study, you should be in a better position to make decisions regarding your study.

The literature review section is a structured review of articles that have been published in academic journals and elsewhere that provide insights into the "how to" issues associated with your study. It is *not* an examination of the company or the competition. For example, a customer satisfaction study for a company like Dick's Sporting Goods doesn't need to focus on Dick's or other sporting goods firms for this section. You would want to find articles that looked at factors that affect customer satisfaction in a retail setting. Similarly, someone looking at customer satisfaction among patients of a given hospital might define hospitals as primarily a service business and expand the review to include studies that examine the measurement of customer satisfaction in service-oriented businesses.

The review of the literature should be organized to include the following sections:

* Conceptual definition

* Methodology

* Measures

* Determinants of customer satisfaction (for customer satisfaction studies)/segmentation variables (for market segmentation studies)

As a result of your review of the relevant literature, you should be able to develop a summary of the current state of knowledge regarding your topic. For example, if you discover that there is a consensus on how to measure the construct, report that with appropriate evidence that points to the consensus. If you find otherwise, you should discuss the approaches that you've identified. The *Publication Manual* of the American Psychological Association (2001, p. 16)[1] provides some useful guidelines for the literature review:

* Do not include an exhaustive historical review.

* Assume the reader is knowledgeable about the field.

- Cite and reference only works pertinent to the specific issue and not works of only general significance.
- Emphasize pertinent findings and relevant methodological issues.

As you conduct the literature review, you should be clear that its purpose is to help you develop a working understanding of methodological issues that are specifically related to the particular type of study you are conducting. In other words, the methodology for a concept study is somewhat different from that for a satisfaction study. It will be helpful for you to become familiar with the methodology generally used for your particular type of study. This section is for your development and is likely to be of little interest to your client. Your instructor may advise you to omit this section from your final report to the client.

Conceptual Definition

Suppose a researcher has decided to study the hypothesis that members of certain groups are more likely to engage in "aggressive behavior" than are members of other groups. The researcher needs to be clear about what is meant by aggressive behavior. Would a young soccer player who aggressively pursues the ball be guilty of aggressive behavior? What about a young child who is the class bully, constantly picking on smaller classmates?

While both may be examples of aggressive behavior, they clearly are very different. Since there has been a great deal of research on the topic of aggression, the researcher would do well to review it, paying careful attention to the definitions other researchers have used. While the researcher will find that investigators have differed to some extent in their definition of aggression, knowing the definitions others have used will help him or her clarify his or her own concept and later to relate his or her findings to those of others.

In the field of marketing, there are a number of concepts that have become commonplace, terms such as *brand loyalty, brand image, customer satisfaction,* and *awareness.* When the researcher attempts to measure these concepts in a way that is meaningful and valid, it is necessary to be precise, defining what is included in the definition and what is excluded. For example, the term *customer satisfaction* has been described in at least two different ways: transaction-specific and cumulative. Viewed as a transaction-specific concept, customer satisfaction refers to an evaluative judgment of a specific purchase. Cumulative customer satisfaction refers to an overall evaluation of the total purchase and consumption experience. Understanding the different conceptualizations that have been used would give the novice researcher insights into the measurement task that would otherwise be missing. Identifying in a clear and definitive way what is meant by a given concept for your study is the first step in the development of appropriate measures.

This section should examine how others have defined the construct (customer satisfaction or attitude or market segmentation). Knowledge of various definitions will allow you to define the term better for your study. We regularly use terms such as *loyalty, satisfaction,* and *heavy user* that, in order to have meaning and be measured, need to be defined. This section will serve to inform you as you prepare to develop your measurements. If there is a consensus on the definition, report that; if there is not, examine the similarities and differences among the various definitions.

This section should probably be a paragraph or two and should examine the definitions from at least four different articles.

Methodology

Is there a standard method for conducting this particular type of study? Have you found, for example, that each study you've identified has used a mail questionnaire or personal interviewing? Perhaps structured, nondisguised questionnaires have been used in each study you've examined. Do these studies tend to utilize large probability samples, or do they tend to be qualitative studies that have smaller samples but utilize depth-interviewing techniques? While the answers to these questions don't require you to utilize the same methodology, they do provide a fairly good basis for the decisions you make in your situation.

This section should report the various methodologies that have been used in the studies you have examined and the reasons for those methodology decisions. Structure this section around data collection techniques (mail, online, telephone, personal) as well as sampling decisions and questionnaire format. Every article you review should have a section that covers the methodology employed.

This section probably will require two or three pages and should include references to at least four different articles.

Measures

Is there a standard scale used to measure customer satisfaction, brand loyalty, perceived quality, or attitude toward a brand? Identifying measures that have been validated in multiple studies provides the researcher with access to proven measures. Given the many available marketing measurement scales for most marketing constructs, the researcher is well advised to use available measures. A good source for identifying measures of a wide variety of marketing-related constructs is *Marketing Scales Handbook* by Gordon Bruner II and Paul Hensel.[2] This handbook is available in most college libraries. It includes a wide range of scales that have been organized around three major groupings: consumer behavior–related scales, sales force and organizational scales, and advertising-related scales.

Often a scale is widely cited and used. Parasuraman, Zeithaml, and Berry (1988)[3] report on a scale (SERVQUAL) designed to measure perceptions of service quality. As you evaluate alternative scales, discuss the procedures that the author or authors used in the design and validation of the measurement instrument and the appropriateness of the measures used for your study.

The purpose of this section is to serve as the basis for your decisions regarding scale construction. By examining how other researchers have measured the construct and identifying appropriate measurement scales that have been validated, you should be better suited to judge the quality and availability of a measurement scale and, if need be, to develop your own.

Determinants of Customer Satisfaction/Segmentation Variables

If you were interested in measuring the satisfaction level of a customer who has purchased a new Lexus RX 330, would you ask only about how satisfied the individual was with the styling of the car? Of course not. You'd like an assessment of the handling, mechanical quality, comfort, features, and so on. What should be included, and what is not a key determinant? This section should examine the relative dimensions or components of the variable. The measurement of customer satisfaction should include a review of product brochures, *Consumer Reports* reviews, articles in trade magazines and newspapers, and other sources that focus on an in-depth review of the product (see www.jdpower.com). In addition to literature searches, you may utilize experience surveys, which would include discussions with appropriate individuals with special expertise such as sales representatives, dealers, and others who may offer some ideas and insights. These determinants or dimensions will serve as the components of your questionnaire.

This section should be presented in list form in a manner similar to the following example borrowed from the J.D. Power Web site.

Customer Satisfaction Determinants

- Mechanical quality
- Feature and accessory quality
- Performance
- Comfort
- Style

For each determinant, there may be a number of questions that will examine specific aspects. For example, comfort may refer to the legroom, the comfort of the seats, the temperature controls, and the headroom. You would be likely to ask a separate question for each.

If you are conducting a segmentation study, your task is to determine the appropriate segmentation variables rather than determinants of satisfaction. The marketer's task is to identify market segments and to decide which one or ones to target. There are many ways by which markets may be segmented. Some researchers look at consumer characteristics: geographic, demographic, and psychographic. Other researchers form segments by examining product usage and consumer responses to benefits. An examination of studies that report on market segmentation efforts should provide key insights into this task.

The Assignment

The literature review section is a review of the relevant articles you have used to familiarize yourself with your research topic. The main goals of this section are to develop your familiarity with the topic and the methodological issues associated with it and to convey in a succinct manner, without sacrificing clarity, the current state of research practice for this topic. This section is intended to provide you with the foundation necessary to make informed decisions with regard to the methodological issues involved in your study and to convey those decisions credibly to the reader. This section of the project will probably run approximately five pages.

Be sure to cite your sources. When you cite authors in the text of your paper, APA format permits you to enclose the authors' last names and the year of publication in parentheses, as in A below, or to use their names in the sentence itself, as in B.

A. "One source of unrealistic images of older people in marketing are the world views of young adults who dominate the creative output of marketing agencies (Lee, 1995)."[4]

B. "Moschis (2003) provides an overview of the opportunities and challenges facing corporate America due to the aging marketplace."[5]

In general, form A is the preferred approach. Your narrative should be about the finding, not about the authors. Occasionally however, you might want to focus on the authors. If so, form B is the preferred approach. These formats should not be intermixed randomly. Consider the objective of the sentence before deciding which choice to make.

Sources

Use the online sources available to you through your library. The following databases should prove extremely useful.

- InfoTrac OneFile
- LexisNexis Academic
- ABI/INFORM Global

You should be utilizing articles that come from journals such as the *Journal of Marketing, Journal of Retailing,* and *Journal of Marketing Services* as well as trade publications, product brochures, publications such as *Consumer Reports,* and online research reports such as J.D. Power.

Notes

1. American Psychological Association. (2001). *Publication Manual of the American Psychological Association* (5th ed.). Washington, D.C.

2. Bruner, G.C., Hensel, P.J. (1994) *Marketing Scales Handbook: A Compilation of Multi-Item Measures.* Chicago: American Marketing Association.

3. Parasuraman, A., Zeithaml, V.A., Berry, L.L. (1988). "SERVQUAL: A Multiple-Item Scale for Measuring Consumer Perceptions of Service Quality." *Journal of Retailing,* Vol. 64, Spring, pp. 12–37.

4. Lee, R.A. (1995). *Ageism in Advertising.* Roseville, MN: High-Yield Advertising.

5. Moschis, G.P. (2003). "Marketing to Older Adults: An Updated Overview of Present Knowledge and Practice." *Journal of Consumer Marketing,* Vol. 20, No. 6, pp. 516–525.

CHAPTER 6

Methodology

Introduction

Suppose *General Motors* is considering a customer satisfaction study to allow it to evaluate its dealership network. Consider some of the questions that would need to be answered before data collection could begin. Who is to be considered a customer? Anyone who enters a dealership? Anyone who has purchased a GM car within a specified time period? Anyone who is considered the primary driver? If a parent purchases a vehicle for a child, who is the customer? Should customers be defined as individuals, or should they be defined as a family unit? What characteristics of these customers should be measured? Are we interested in their age and gender, or perhaps where they live? When should we measure them: while they are in the showroom, one week after they have purchased, one month? Should we measure the same customers once (cross-sectional) or more than once (longitudinal)?

How shall we measure? Shall we use a questionnaire, or shall we observe their behavior? If we use a questionnaire, what form will it take? Will it be highly structured? Disguised? How will it be administered: personal interview, telephone, mail, online?

Each of these questions is concerned with the methodology that will be utilized in your project. Questions regarding the population of interest and who should be studied are issues of methodology that will be addressed separately in Chapter 8, where we are concerned with the sampling plan. While some of the answers to these questions will be self-evident, others will not be readily apparent. The researcher needs to base the answers on clear judgments. The rationales for the decisions have to be provided as well.

This section of your research project focuses on the methodologies selected, issues such as those discussed above. It provides insights into your plans and gives the potential client the basis upon which to judge your project.

Primary Data Collection Methods

A number of different methods can be utilized in the collection of primary data. Two broad approaches to the collection of primary data are often labeled as questioning and observation. In the questioning approach respondents are active participants, whereas in the observation approach they do not directly verbally communicate with the researcher. The questioning method generally is considered better suited for situations in which information regarding a respondent's demographic/socioeconomic characteristics, attitudes, opinions, and lifestyles may be gathered. Observation may be preferred when the researcher seeks to obtain information about behavior and certain demographic characteristics.

To put the two approaches into the proper perspective, it is useful to mention two points. First, one approach is not necessarily a substitute for the other. Certain situations may call for one approach or the other. For example, a study that was interested in understanding young children's reaction to a new toy almost certainly would utilize an observation methodology rather than a questioning approach. Second, the advantages that are mentioned in your text for each approach do not hold true in every situation. Neither approach can be held out as the universally preferred approach.

While each approach has advantages and disadvantages compared with the other and would be preferred for selected types of studies, the studies that are described in Chapter 2 probably would call for some version of a questioning study. Therefore, the remainder of this chapter will focus on the decisions that are associated with studies that use a questioning approach. This section of your project should address the specific issues associated with primary data collection. Specifically, address the methods that you plan to use to collect the data. If a questioning methodology is to be used, you'll need to determine which technique will best suit your situation. You will find that there is not a single best method. Each technique has its uses, and none is superior in all situations.

Questioning Methodology

A number of decisions need to be made in order to implement a *questioning* methodology. As you develop your data collection plan, you should consider each of these decision issues. Remember that there are always trade-offs that have to be evaluated when you are considering different research methods. Your text details many of these issues, and you need to consider the advantages and disadvantages of each one in the context of your research problem. The choices that you make should take a number of factors into account, including (1) the information needs of the study, (2) the budgetary resources available, (3) the time available, and (4) access to the population to be studied.

Collecting the data using a *questioning* methodology requires contact with the respondents, which can be accomplished in various ways. Thus, one decision that needs to be made revolves around the contact method to be utilized.

Two methods of data collection utilize an interview procedure:

1. One-to-one personal interview of the respondent

2. Interviewing respondents by telephone

Two methods rely on self-administered questionnaires:

1. Online (e-mail, Web)

2. Mail (fax)

A *personal interview* is a face-to-face conversation between the interviewer and the respondent. If you intend to utilize a personal interviewing methodology for your study, be sure to address the following two issues: *(1) Where will the interviews be conducted?* and *(2) How will respondents be selected?*

The interview most often takes place in a central location such as a shopping mall (called a mall intercept method) but can take place in a home or office. The personal interview allows the use of open-ended questions that require extensive probing, an advantage over the telephone (which may utilize limited use of probing) and mail (which does not lend itself to such questions). Consumer studies that use a mall intercept suffer from the inability to target selected sampling units. This method tends to overrepresent the types of people who frequent these areas, introducing the potential for bias. However, when select populations (accountants, human resources managers, doctors, etc.) are the group of interest, a personal interview allows the interviewer to select respondents from a list available from trade directories. The interviewer can contact the selected respondent and arrange a mutually acceptable time for the interview to take place. In this situation and in others in which the sample elements are selected objectively, personal interviewing represents a reasonable opportunity to select a representative sample and secure the cooperation of the designated respondent.

The *telephone interview* is usually (but not always) a relatively short interview (a few minutes). Telephone interviewing allows for follow-up questions and probing. Computer-assisted interviewing software has helped make telephone interviews the most popular data collection technique, increasing the speed and flexibility of this method. Telephone interviews are particularly appropriate when the population of interest is dispersed across a large geographic area and when the turnaround time needs to be short. Despite the wide use of telephone interviewing, the method does have some disadvantages. It is not appropriate when visual aids are needed or when the interview has to explore a number of topics in depth. An increase in the number of cell phones, particularly for the age group 18 to 30 has made it increasingly difficult to reach younger respondents. Unlisted phone numbers, answering machines, and caller ID used to screen calls make it difficult to get to live consumers, but a persistent researcher who calls back at different times generally will be able to make contact. When contact is made, in order to secure cooperation, it is important to assure the respondent that there will be no effort to sell anything and that the responses will be kept confidential.

TABLE 6.1 Ranking of Questionnaire Administration Methods for Selected Criteria

Criteria	Personal	Telephone	Mail	Online
Speed	3	2	4	1
Low cost	4	3	2	1
Sampling control	1	2	3	4
Information needs: length of questionnaire	1	4	2	3

Note: The comparative ratings shown in this table are not universal; exceptions to these rankings occur, depending on the circumstances surrounding a research situation.

Self-administered questionnaires that are administered through the *mail* or *online* via e-mail or the Web are generally the least expensive. While the response time for mail questionnaires is generally the longest, the response time for e-mail or Web-based surveys may be very short. Self-administered questionnaires allow the respondent to work at his or her own pace and are free from interviewer bias. Mail questionnaires have the ability to reach a wide audience with sampling frames that are easily developed and costs that are relatively low. However, the response rate for mail questionnaires is the lowest of all these methods, and the researcher has little control in securing responses from the designated individual. Mail questionnaires are the slowest of the major methods in terms of completion time.

Online questionnaires may have a short response time but do not work well when a general population is of interest. There are a number of online survey software products (some that are distributed with major textbooks) that allow the researcher to create online surveys and distribute them over the Internet. You can find descriptions of two of those products at SurveyTime.com and WebSurveyor.com. While there continues to be concern about the representativeness of respondents who are generally self-selected for online surveys, it is clear that the speed and low cost of online surveys as well as the relatively high quality of the data will ensure that online surveys are here to stay.

Each of the four basic methods—personal interview, telephone, group interview, mail, and online—has its own specific advantages and disadvantages. The decision as to which method will be used is crucial to the project and will result in a project very different from what would follow from a different methodology. The methodologies differ in many ways, although basic differences among the four methods lie in the intensity of interaction between the respondent and the interviewer and the accessibility to respondents. Other differences of note are the data collection costs and the data collection time required. Your textbook has a comparison of the methods with regard to a number of criteria. Using the criteria described in your text and the information needs you have identified for your project, evaluate each method in terms of appropriateness for your study. You should be able to explain your rationale for the selection of one method over another based on these criteria (Table 6.1).

Project Decision: Which data collection contact method will you utilize? Explain why.

Question Format

A decision with regard to data collection contact methodology has implications for the degree of structure of the questionnaire. *Structure* refers to the extent to which the questions and answers are standardized. A questionnaire that utilizes questions with predetermined responses would be considered highly structured. Structured questions are simple to administer and easy to analyze. Unstructured questions tend to be predetermined in only general terms, and the respondent is free to answer in his or her own words. Unstructured questions are generally more difficult to analyze but offer the advantage of potentially gaining more insight into the respondent's true feelings. While a questionnaire may utilize both structured and unstructured questions, your decision regarding the method of administration has implications for the decision about the degree of structure. Mail and online questionnaires are generally structured, while personal and telephone interviews tend to be predominantly structured with some unstructured questions.

Project Decision: What degree of structure will characterize your questionnaire? Will you utilize structured questions or unstructured or a combination of each? Why?

Getting Cooperation

Marketing researchers have noticed a steady decline in survey cooperation in recent years. While telephone surveys are the most commonly used method, attempts to reach a representative sample face a number of potential problems. Cell phones, unlisted telephones, answering machines, and caller ID are especially problematic as each represents a significant hurdle for researchers attempting to secure a representative sample. Online surveys are very effective for reaching specialized audiences but are not usually appropriate for a general audience. Mail surveys are generally least effective in terms of generating a high response rate, and those who do respond are often significantly different from the nonrespondents. The personal interview method is best suited for reaching an appropriate audience and securing a high rate of cooperation. The disadvantage of this method is largely one of cost. Since your project is likely to use members of your group rather than professional interviewers to conduct the interviews, cost may not be a significant issue.

Regardless of the data collection method chosen, you will need to consider actions that you can take to ensure a high rate of participation in your study. Discuss your plans to secure the participation of the selected respondents. A partial list of actions designed to secure participation follows:

1. Attempt to convince respondents of the value of the research and the importance of their participation.

2. Provide advance notice that the survey is coming.

3. Use personalized cover letters.

4. Use random-digit dialing procedures to represent households with unlisted telephones.

5. Use first-class mail, follow-up questionnaires, and small incentives—monetary or nonmonetary—to increase the response rate in mail questionnaires.

6. Guarantee anonymity.

7. Call back at another time, preferably at a different time of the day.

8. Avoid interesting but not vital questions.

9. Carefully select participants for whom the topic has relevance.

Project Decision: What actions will you take to ensure adequate cooperation by selected study participants? Explain.

The Assignment

This is an important part of your research project. It requires a great deal of planning and careful evaluation of a number of alternatives with regard to selected criteria. Everything that occurs in the later stages of your study will be dependent on the decisions that are made here. In this section of your report you should describe your plans for data collection. The plans should be specific (for example, if you plan on using a personal interview, where will the interviews be conducted, what times of day, and how will cooperation be secured?) and should discuss the rationale for your decision. Focus your decisions around the questions below.

Primary Data Collection Methods

- What data collection contact methodology will you use? Why?

- What level of structure will you utilize in your questionnaire? Why?

- What steps will you take to enhance participation in your study? Explain.

Note: Many instructors may want you to include your sampling plan in this section. Others may prefer that the sampling plan be presented separately. Refer to Chapter 8 for a discussion of sampling.

CHAPTER 7

Questionnaire Design

Introduction

Based on the work you have completed to this point, you are ready to construct the questionnaire. Be sure to refer back to what you have done in both the *research objectives and information needs* section and the *methodology* section as you begin to develop the questionnaire. While textbooks present questionnaire development as sequential, following a step-by-step process, it is really an iterative process. You may need to return to the questionnaire to modify it after you have considered sampling and data analysis issues. While following a structured step-by-step process in questionnaire design is not always possible, a beginning researcher may find a set of steps helpful. Whether the survey is self-administered, such as a mail or online survey, or is an interview survey, such as telephone or personal interview, the same principles of questionnaire design generally apply.

The questionnaire usually has at least three sections, each serving a different purpose. The first section introduces the survey. Since survey participation is entirely voluntary, the introduction section is intended to secure participation. Those who refuse to participate do so within the first few seconds after initial contact, whether the survey is administered by mail, telephone, in person, or online. Those who begin rarely withdraw their cooperation and usually complete the questionnaire. If the questionnaire is introduced properly, the response rate will be increased and the reliability and validity of the results will be improved.

The second section of the questionnaire contains the questions that are designed to measure the survey topics. The third section includes questions that measure characteristics of the respondent. This chapter provides a brief review of the stages of questionnaire design, with attention given to specific issues to be considered at each stage. It also includes a section that addresses common student concerns about the organization of the questionnaire.

The Process

1. Specify what information is needed.
2. Determine the type of questionnaire and method of administration.
3. Determine the content of individual questions.
4. Determine the form of response to each question.
5. Determine the wording of each question.
6. Determine the question sequence.
7. Design the layout.
8. Reexamine and revise.
9. Pretest and revise if necessary.

While the stages of development generally are presented as sequential, in practice they typically tend to involve an iterative process. It's likely that you will work back and forth among some of the stages and will develop multiple drafts of your questionnaire. Be creative in your approach and pretest the questionnaire to determine whether the typical respondent understands each question and is willing and able to supply the information you are seeking.

Determine What Information You Need

The first two steps should have been completed already. When you handed in the list of *research objectives and information needs,* you identified what information you would be seeking for this project. That list, perhaps revised as a result of your instructor's comments, will serve as the basis for your questionnaire. Make sure the questionnaire is designed in a way that satisfies each of your objectives and provides the information you have determined is needed. Each question on the questionnaire should be cross-checked against the information needs. Each should be clearly identified as meeting a specific need. As you proceed, you may identify questions that are not related to any information need. You may want to cut those questions. Likewise, you may identify gaps in your questionnaire where no question was developed to address a particular research objective or information need. It is better to fix that problem in the design stage than it is to discover it after the questionnaire has been administered.

Determine the Method of Administration and Questionnaire Type

In the *methodology* section, the type of questionnaire and the method of administration were specified. It is important that questionnaire design follow and not precede the methodology section. Clearly, the data collection method will be a critical influence on the wording and structure of a questionnaire. A personal interview is likely to be more conducive to unstructured-undisguised open-ended questions. A mail questionnaire generally does not utilize open-ended questions.

Determine the Content of Individual Questions

If you have developed a clear list of the information needs for your study, you have already identified key issues associated with individual questions. Additionally, you should consider the following questions:

- *Is this question necessary*? If the information has already been captured by another question, there may be no reason to cover it again. If you do not have plans to use this question in your analysis, the question may not be necessary.

- *Are several questions needed to address different dimensions*? There may be situations in which the respondents could answer differently based on the frame of reference. For example, you may be interested in a customer's evaluation of the transaction and the experience of using the product. Both may address customer satisfaction, but from different perspectives.

- *Can the respondent answer*? Examine each question to determine whether the typical respondent could be expected to have the information necessary to answer the question in a meaningful way. The world is a complicated place, and the respondent probably knows a lot about some things and a little about others. Is this a question that requires information that the typical respondent may not have?

- *Will the respondent answer*? Is this question asking for information that is of a personal nature? Perhaps the answer may involve a great deal of effort. For example, asking an open-ended question in a mail questionnaire probably will result in a shorthand answer that does not fully reflect the respondent's attitude.

Determine the Form of the Response to the Question

Once you have determined the content of the question, you'll need to decide on the form of the response. Will the respondents be free to answer in their own words, or will they choose the alternative that most closely resembles their position on the subject? In an *open-ended question* the respondent replies in his or her own words. This form often is used in the beginning of the questionnaire as a general question that may offer some insight into a respondent's frame of reference or as a follow-up question that seeks elaboration of a respondent's reply.

A fixed alternative question may be dichotomous (two choices) or multichotomous (more than two choices). Respondents may be presented with a number of alternatives and asked to select the alternative that best reflects their position.

The literature review you conducted earlier in the semester should be helpful at this stage. Check out the form of the questions that were reported in the studies you have reviewed. While you may decide on a form different from that of the reported studies, at least you'll get a good idea of how others have decided to formulate comparable questions.

A few examples that show alternative question formats may help illustrate some of your choices. The *Marketing Scales Handbook* by Bruner and Hensel, published by the American Marketing Association and mentioned in Chapter 3, includes over 500 multi-item marketing scales. Among the many scales, there are at least 13 different scales for measuring "satisfaction," scales that measure the degree of satisfaction with products (car), services (air travel), purchases in general, and even life. As you review the following scales, notice how they differ. The first and third scales are unforced, while the second is a forced scale. The first scale uses only three category descriptors, while the second and fourth use a descriptor for each category. These scales are examples of those which are typically used in marketing studies.

Satisfaction (Car)

A 12-item, seven-point Likert-type summated rating scale that measured a consumer's degree of satisfaction with a car.

Strongly Agree			Neither			Strongly Disagree
1	2	3	4	5	6	7

Three of the 12 items are shown below.

1. This is one of the best cars I could have bought.
2. This car is exactly what I need.
3. This car hasn't worked out as well as I thought it would.

Satisfaction (Air Travel)

A four-item, six-point Likert-type scale that measures the degree to which a person expresses satisfaction with air travel.

Strongly Disagree	Disagree	Slightly Disagree	Slightly Agree	Agree	Strongly Agree
1	2	3	4	5	6

1. I choose to travel by airline because my time is very valuable to me.
2. I feel the services I receive during the flight are good.
3. I feel that the preflight services (i.e., baggage handling, ticket processing) are good.
4. Normally, I fly with one particular airline company.

Satisfaction (Generalized)

A six-item, semantic differential scale measuring a consumer's degree of satisfaction with an object. (Three items of the six are shown below.)

Please indicate how *satisfied* you were with* (insert the object toward which satisfaction is being measured) by checking the space that best gives your answer.

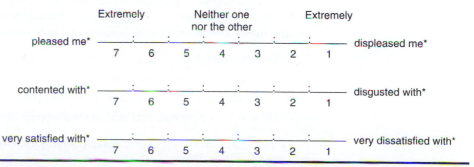

Convenience (Locating Products within a Store)

A five-item, five-point summated rating scale that measures the degree of importance a consumer places on ease of finding products in a store.

Not Important	Below-Average Importance	Average Importance	Above-Average Importance	Very Important
1	2	3	4	5

1. Knowledgeable salespersons
2. Help in finding items in store
3. Ease of finding items
4. Small store so items can be found easily
5. Limited variety so items can be found easily

These examples illustrate a few of the alternative formats that may be used within your questionnaire.

Decide on the Wording of Each Question

This is an important task in the development of your questionnaire because poor phrasing of a question can distort your findings significantly. Your textbook provides some basic rules of thumb to consider and some examples of how a single word can change the meaning of a question. Pay careful attention to your choice of wording and test the questions to determine that they are interpreted the way you intend. For the purposes of this project, you can do a quick pretest by asking friends, classmates, or others to read the questions and talk out loud as they fill them in. You'll be particularly interested in their interpretation of the questions and the degree to which the questionnaire flows. Questions that are ambiguous, confusing, or difficult to answer should be identified in the pretest and modified. You'll be surprised to find that some questions that were clear to you after having worked on them for weeks may be a source of confusion for others. It is better to uncover the problems before the questionnaire is distributed to your sample.

Probably the most important principle regarding question wording is that only one concept or issue should be included in a question. Your text may refer to this by providing the advice to avoid "double-barreled questions." To interpret the respondent's answer, you need to know what he or she is referring to. When a question includes more than one concept, the respondent may answer regarding one or both or do some melding of the concepts. A few examples that illustrate how not to formulate questions follow:

- "Are you satisfied with the level of service in the bar and the restaurant?"
- "How likely would you be to vote for someone who is a Democrat and an atheist?"

Clearly, in the first case an individual could be satisfied with service in the bar but not in the restaurant, or vice versa, and in the second case the concepts of political party and religious beliefs are combined. In both cases the researcher would not be able to interpret the answer clearly.

A second important principle is to avoid using ambiguous words. For example, the use of the word *convenience* in a study regarding a retail shopping district may have a variety of meanings. Convenience could mean any of the following:

- "The shopping district is located close to my home."
- "The shopping district is open nights and weekends."
- "There are a wide variety of stores in the shopping district."
- "There is ample parking available in the shopping district."

Be clear and be precise as you develop your questions.

Determine the Question Sequence

If you have determined the question form and the specific wording for each question, it is time to put the questions together into a questionnaire. Again, the best advice comes in the form of some general rules of thumb. A few of these rules follow:

- The first few questions should be simple, easy to answer, nonthreatening, and interesting.
- There should be a logical order to the questions. Start with broad questions and progressively narrow the scope.
- Place sensitive questions later in the questionnaire.
- Place the classification (demographic/socioeconomic) questions last.
- Questions that are not relevant to certain respondents should be skipped. Carefully sequence questionnaire items to present a clear and easy-to-follow skip pattern.

Determine the Layout

The questionnaire layout can affect respondents' reactions to the questionnaire, interviewers' ability to utilize the questionnaire appropriately, and ultimately the accuracy of the replies. Pay careful attention to the appearance of the questionnaire. If it is important for individuals to take the time to answer it, it is important that the appearance be neat, and that it has been carefully edited to ensure there are no spelling or grammatical errors.

For most surveys, the questions can be grouped into sections that make the task appear easier for the respondent. Effectively grouping questions into sections enhances the efficiency of the questionnaire. There are three means of grouping items:

- *Grouping items by topic.* Suppose you are measuring customer satisfaction with an automobile and have identified the determinants of customer satisfaction to be mechanical quality, feature and accessory quality, performance, comfort, and style. It would make sense to ask all the questions about various aspects of mechanical quality in one section and then ask about each of the other determinants in subsequent sections.
- *Grouping items by scaling techniques.* It is common to see different scaling techniques in the same questionnaire. When that is the case, it may be practical to include all the questions that utilize a given scale in one section. Perhaps you have a number of questions that use a Likert scale (Strongly Agree, Agree, Neutral, Disagree, Strongly Disagree). Grouping these questions in one section allows you to list the items as statements and place the scale at the top of the section, showing it only once. Likewise, if another section uses a satisfaction scale (Very Satisfied, Satisfied, Neutral, Dissatisfied, Very Dissatisfied), you can group the items as a list and provide the instructions and the scale at the top of the section. The respondent needs to read the instructions only once and can proceed more easily through the section.
- *Grouping items both ways.* Perhaps the best approach is to group items by both topic and scale types. A set of items that address the same topic may use the same scale. Grouping by both scale and topic provides a logical sequence that should allow for greater efficiencies in terms of respondent time and utilization of space on the questionnaire.

Questionnaire Introduction   Regardless of the method with which the survey will be administered, online or mail, personal or telephone, an effective introduction will increase the response rate. An ineffective introduction has the effect of increasing nonresponse error, threatening the validity of the findings. Remember, cooperation on the part of respondents is entirely voluntary. The introduction section of the questionnaire needs to explain the purpose of the questionnaire and why the respondent should take the time to cooperate. Ideally, the introduction will arouse the respondent's curiosity and interest about the nature of the questions to follow. A hospital marketing survey may be introduced as a "study of new health-care services." A political questionnaire may be introduced as a "study of important issues facing the community." Keep the introduction as brief as possible, giving the respondent little opportunity to refuse.

In the case of mail surveys, the cover letter serves the purpose of introducing the study. Everything in your cover letter is designed to convince respondents of the need to cooperate. A good cover letter will state the importance of the research project, the purpose of the study, and the importance of the respondent's participation. It should include an identification of the sender's organization (generally without identifying the sponsor), a promise that replies will remain confidential, and a mention of how the respondent was selected and should include a small token of appreciation and a request for a quick reply. These features apply to online surveys as well. The challenge for the online survey is to convince potential respondents to visit the Web site containing the online survey. The online invitation needs to be concise and convincing and shares many of the same features of a good cover letter.

With personal and telephone questionnaires, the introduction needs to quickly convince respondents of the importance of the research and their participation. Included in the introduction should be the following:

- An appropriate greeting such as "Good afternoon! I am Tim Stevens from Lakeside Research Associates."

- A brief statement about the project and its purpose such as "We are conducting a survey of area residents regarding their feelings toward the hospital."

- An indication of how long the interview might last such as "This should take no more than ten minutes."

- A polite request for permission to conduct the interview such as "May I please talk to you for a few minutes."

Questionnaire Instructions   For each set of questions or items, you should include *instructions* that tell the respondent or the interviewer how the response should be provided. For self-administered questionnaires, such as mail or online, the instructions should take into account the complexity of the scaling technique. The following examples are taken from *The Marketing Scales Handbook* and are used to demonstrate various types of instructions that may be used depending on the complexity of the scale. In some cases, such as the commonly used Likert scale with five categories that range from "Strongly Agree" to "Strongly Disagree," the instructions may be as simple as *"Please indicate your opinion by checking one response for each statement"* or *"Please indicate how much you agree or disagree with each statement."*

Other scales that are more complex may require greater elaboration. For example, the following instructions are for a scale that was designed to measure the degree of commitment to one's profession. The scale is a three-item, seven-point Likert scale: *"Listed below are a number of statements which involve possible feelings about working in one's profession or field of expertise. With respect to your own feelings about the field of expertise in which you now work, please use the following scale to indicate the extent of agreement or disagreement. There are no right or wrong answers."* In another case where the scale was designed to measure attitude toward an advertisement, the following instructions were provided: *"Please tell us how well you think each of the words listed below describes the ad you have just seen by putting a number to the right of the word. Here we are interested in your thoughts about the ad, not the brand or product class. If you think the word describes the ad extremely well, put a 5; very well, put a 4; fairly well, put a 3; not very well, put a 2; not well at all, put a 1."*

As you can see, the length and complexity of the instructions will vary. Properly worded instructions should do the following:

- Identify the question or items they pertain to

- Provide the criterion or standard to be used

- Explain how to use the scale

- Explain exactly how and where to place the responses

The Assignment

You will go over in class many of the issues associated with questionnaire design. While there are a number of guidelines that you will learn, ultimately the design of a good questionnaire is probably more art than science. *For this section, you will need to include a finished copy of your questionnaire and a list that identifies the information need that each question satisfies.*

As you review your questionnaire, consider the following questions taken from the project score sheet:

- Does the questionnaire cover the necessary information that was listed in the information needs section?
- Is the wording simple yet clear?
- Does the questionnaire avoid leading or biasing questions?
- Are the questions properly sequenced?
- Have the questions anticipated the ability of the respondent to respond accurately?
- Has the questionnaire been introduced properly?
- Does the questionnaire contain clear instructions and an attractive layout?

CHAPTER 8

The Sampling Plan

Introduction

Sampling is the selection of a subset of the population of interest for the purpose of drawing conclusions about the entire population. In class you will discuss the advantages of sampling over a census, the differences between probability sampling and nonprobability sampling, how to determine sample size, and much more. In this section of your proposal you need to provide a detailed plan that specifies the population, states the desired sample size, discusses the sampling strategy to be employed with an accompanying rationale, and identifies a viable sampling frame.

Population

Population refers to the totality of cases that conform to some designated specifications. In addition to people, it may refer to retail stores, manufacturing firms, or even objects such as inventory items. The designated specifications are needed to identify who (or what) belongs to the targeted group and who doesn't. A study aimed at establishing a profile of shoppers in a downtown shopping district requires specification of who is considered a shopper. Anyone who has ever shopped in the downtown area, who has shopped with a given frequency, or has purchased a given dollar amount in a month? A week?

Researchers need to be very explicit in defining the target group. The definition should not only identify who is in the group but also be precise enough to distinguish those who are not in the targeted group. One way to define the population of interest is to include the following components:

- *Element*. This is the unit of interest. The population is the aggregate of all the elements. If a poll was taken to estimate the likely winner of the presidential election, the element may be defined as the registered voter, the likely voter, or the voter who voted in the last election. Note that the element is a single unit. The population would then be the aggregate of all the registered voters in the state or in the nation. In a study designed to describe the profile of the typical listener of a public radio station, the element is the *listener*. In your study the element, for example, may be defined as an individual who has purchased a given quantity over a specified time period or a person who is the primary household user.

- *Sampling unit*. This is the element that is available for selection during the sampling process. For example, in the public radio station study the element was defined as listeners of the station. However, since there was no economical way to identify everyone who regularly listened to the station, the sampling unit was defined as those who were members of the station, meaning they made financial contributions. The station had a database of members, making them easily accessible. It was not ideal but in a practical sense was probably the best that could be done. The study needs to explain clearly the differences that may exist between the element and the sampling unit.

- *Extent*. This defines the geographic boundaries. For example, customers for a given store may be defined as living within the 13126 Zip code area, living within a 10-mile radius of the store, or living in New York State. A pollster may define the population as "likely voters who live in New York." Sometimes a target population may not be bounded by geography as in the case of e-commerce, but more often than not it is.

- *Time.* If the study is cross-sectional, it is at best a snapshot of the population at a point in time. Define the time period. You often hear the pollster say something like "If the election were held today, candidate X would defeat the incumbent." That recognizes the fluid nature of such studies and the fact that attitudes change over time. By including this component to your population definition you are acknowledging the changes that occur normally as a function of time.

This section should be presented as follows:

Element

Sampling unit

Extent

Time

Sampling Frame

The sampling frame is the list of elements from which the actual sample will be drawn. Say the target population for a study is all the households in the metropolitan Syracuse area. The Syracuse phone book would seem to be an easy and good example of a sampling frame. However, on further examination it becomes clear that the telephone directory would not include those with unlisted phones or those who recently moved into the area.

Rarely will the researcher find a perfect match between the defined population and the sampling frame. When the list of population elements is not readily available, the researcher will need to develop an appropriate sampling frame. This may mean that several lists are combined and then purified with regard to overlap and ineligibles. In the case of customer satisfaction studies, the "client" in many cases can be assumed to have a database of customers, perhaps those with charge accounts. But even with such a database, what about the occasional walk-in?

Identifying an appropriate sampling frame can be difficult. If no good list is readily available from the client, the researcher may need to search for commercially available lists. One good source that lists mailing lists and the rates to purchase the lists is *Standard Rate and Data Service—Direct Marketing List Source*.

This section needs to show the steps taken to identify an appropriate list, describe the characteristics of those who are on the list, and compare the characteristics of those on the list to the defined population. If there is a significant discrepancy, a rationale for selecting the designated sampling frame will be needed.

Sampling Procedure

Sampling techniques can be divided into two broad categories of probability and nonprobability samples. In a probability sample, each element of the population has a known, nonzero chance of being included in the sample. Everyone has a known chance of being included, even if the chances are not necessarily equal. With nonprobability samples, there is no known chance that any element in the target population will be included in the sample.

You will have examined in class and the text gives sufficient coverage to the various sample designs for probability and nonprobability samples. Recall that probability samples may be classified as *simple random, stratified,* and *cluster samples,* while nonprobability samples are classified as *convenience, quota, snowball,* and *judgment samples.* It is only when probability samples have been utilized that the precision of the sample results can be assessed. The sampling results from a nonprobability study cannot be used to make statistical inferences about the population, offering only preliminary insights. For this reason, probability samples are generally considered superior, at least to the extent that sampling error can be measured, when the intention is to make inferences to the population.

In this section of your project, *determine the sampling procedure that you will use and explain why this method is superior for this project to other methods* that were considered.

Sample Size

You have learned various methods for determining sample size. Those methods have required that you make a few assumptions or decisions with regard to desired precision, confidence level, and the variance of the population. In this section you will need to explain the methods you used to determine sample size and show your recommendations regarding sample size.

The determination of sample size is based on a number of considerations. First, analysis considerations may require that sample size be determined from the number of cells in a cross-tabulation. For example, if the critical analysis requires a cross-tabulation of two variables that create nine cells and if it is felt that there should be at least 30 observations in a cell, the absolute minimum sample size needed would be 270.

Second, determining the appropriate sample size requires that the researcher consider the amount of time and money available as well as the level of precision needed. Time and money are often the most critical considerations for student projects. Projects vary greatly at this stage, depending on the instructor's expectations. It is likely that your instructor will expect you to specify a desired level of precision and the sample size necessary to achieve that level. However, you probably will need to acknowledge resource constraints in terms of both time and money to justify the smaller sample you actually will use.

The traditional approach to sample size determination is based on the idea of constructing confidence intervals around the sample mean or proportion. Three factors play a role in the determination of sample size using this traditional approach:

1. *Precision.* The greater the precision, the larger the necessary sample size. How *precise* do you want the sample estimate to be? Think of this as determining the size of the estimating interval. National political polls often claim to be precise to within ± 3 percent. Other times you'll see overnight poll results that may be precise to within ± 5 percent. The degree of precision will be greatly influenced by the importance of the decision involved. If millions of dollars ride on the results of the decision, the acceptable range of error is likely to be quite small.

2. *Confidence level.* You will need to make a decision regarding the confidence level as well. In most cases you'll settle on a 95 percent confidence level; that is, you will want to be 95 percent confident that the population parameter will fall within the confidence interval. The higher the level of confidence is, the larger the sample will need to be.

3. *Estimate of variance.* The greater the variability of the characteristic is, the larger the sample size will need to be. You have learned various ways to handle the estimation of the variance. Past studies would be useful here, but in their absence you may need to make an informed judgment: your best guess. In the case of means, you may estimate the variance by considering that for a normally distributed variable the range of the variable is approximately equal to plus or minus three standard deviations. Thus, if you can estimate the range, you can estimate the standard deviation by dividing by 6.

The interrelationship between these three basic factors can best be illustrated through an example. We will look at the situation for determining sample size when the researcher wishes to estimate a *mean value* within some desired level of precision and the situation when the question is designed to estimate a population *proportion.*

Sample Size Determination When Estimating Means

The following formula may be used for questions designed to estimate the population mean:

$$n = \frac{z^2 \, s^2}{H^2}$$

where:

$$n = \text{required sample size}$$
$$z = \text{desired level of confidence}$$
$$s = \text{estimated standard deviation}$$
$$H = \text{acceptable level of precision}$$

Solving the equation for n requires that you specify the confidence level (z) and the acceptable level of precision (H) and estimate the population standard deviation. If the population standard deviation (s) is known from previous studies, you should use that. More likely, however, is the situation represented in the formula above, in which you need to estimate the standard deviation. Assuming that there are no past studies on which to base your estimate of the population standard deviation (s), you have a few options. You could do a pilot study to get a quick estimate. Another possibility is to use what you know about normally distributed variables, that the range of variation is approximately equal to $\pm$ 3 standard deviations. Thus, if you do not have an estimate of the population standard deviation but can estimate the range of variation, you can estimate the standard deviation by dividing the range by 6.

An acceptable level of precision will consider what the likely population mean is in order to arrive at an acceptable error margin. For example, if you are interested in estimating the average household income of your customers and know that the mean income in your community is $45,000, you probably will be satisfied with a precision of $300 to $500. However, if you were looking to estimate the average expenditure of the typical tourist in your community per day, you probably would be looking at a precision level in the range of $25 to $40.

To illustrate, let us look at an example from a recent student project. The student group was looking at the local market for fitness centers, trying to estimate the potential for a new fitness center close to campus. One key question of the study involved the price students typically paid for fitness center memberships. Specifically, the question posed to students who were members of competing health clubs was "*How much do you pay per semester for your fitness club membership?*"

The student team knew that prices in the community ranged from $150 to $450 per semester. Dividing that range by 6, the student group estimated the standard deviation (s) to be $50. Specifying that the study would use a 95 percent confidence interval ($z = 1.96$) and that the acceptable precision would be $\pm$ $15, the group arrived at an appropriate sample size:

$$n = \frac{z^2 \, s^2}{H^2}$$
$$= \frac{1.96^2 \, 50^2}{15^2}$$
$$= 43$$

The appropriate sample size to deliver the specified precision level for a 95 percent confidence level was 43.

Sample Size Determination When Estimating Proportions

In addition to estimating the average fitness club membership fee, the group was interested in estimating the proportion of the student body that had memberships at fitness centers in the area. Again, they had no previous studies, and so the population standard deviation was unknown. The following formula is used for questions designed to estimate the population proportion:

$$H = z\sigma_p$$

Substituting $\sqrt{p(1 - p)/n}$ for σ_p and solving for n yields

$$n = \frac{z^2 \, p(1 - p)}{H^2}$$

where:

$$n = \text{required sample size}$$

$$z = \text{desired level of confidence}$$

$$p = \text{expected proportion}$$

$$H = \text{acceptable level of precision}$$

If you are estimating a population *proportion,* you'll probably want to consider a desired precision level (customarily denoted as H to signify half precision, i.e., one-half of the confidence interval) between $\pm$ .03 (3 percent) and .05 (5 percent). For a student project in which time and funds are limited, precision probably will be less than it will be in situations where resources are less scarce. In this example, on the basis of a small pilot study, the student group estimated that 20 percent of the student body maintained fitness club memberships. Specifying a precision level of $\pm$ .05 and a 90 percent confidence interval, the group arrived at an appropriate sample size, as shown below:

$$n = \frac{z^2 \; p(1-p)}{H^2}$$

$$= \frac{1.645^2 \; .2(1-.2)}{.05^2}$$

$$= 173$$

This is a typical situation in which one study has multiple objectives. The different objectives of the study produced conflicting sample sizes; n could be 43 or 173. In this example the students needed to reconcile these values to come up with a suitable sample size for the study as a whole. A conservative approach would be to select the larger sample size, ensuring that each of the two variables would be estimated with the required degree of precision. However, if the first question (where $n = 43$) is considered to be the most critical and the second question (where $n = 173$) is secondary, choosing a sample size of 173 will present an unnecessary expense. Focus on the most critical variables, understanding that the other variables may be estimated with less precision than originally desired.

The examples above focused on the determination of sample size using statistical principles based on the assumption that a probability sampling procedure was used.

Sometimes you'll be using *a rating scale,* for instance, a five-point scale or a six-point scale. In those instances you may be interested in reporting the percent that are favorable. For example, a balanced six-point scale that measures the degree to which a person is satisfied with the variety of food offered in the dining hall may be analyzed by combining the favorable responses and reporting the results as a proportion. In that case you could use the formula given for determining sample size when the question is designed to estimate the proportion.

Remember, if you need to determine sample size when estimating a proportion, you will have to make an estimate of the population proportion in order to estimate the variance. The population proportion can be estimated by judgment, based on previous studies, or by the results of a small pilot study. Your estimate of the population proportion will allow you to estimate the population variance. This estimate is likely to be either greater than or less than the actual variance. If your estimate is less than the population variance turns out to be, the confidence interval will be less precise than was desired. Recall that the variance will be estimated by the formula: $s^2 = [p(1-p)]$. The maximum variance is achieved when the sample proportion (p) is equal to .5. Any value of p smaller than .5 will result in a smaller variance. An estimate of $p = .5$ will guarantee that you'll get at least the desired level of precision, and if your estimate is off, your results will be more precise than desired.

The type of sample, the statistic in question, the variance within the population, and the time and money available for the study all make the sample size decision a complex one. You should know that the standard coverage of this subject in marketing research texts applies primarily to simple random samples. The determination of sample size for a stratified or cluster sample is beyond the scope of this manual, and the reader should consult one of the standard references on sampling theory. Sample size formulas cannot be appropriately used in nonprobability samples. As a result, the researcher generally determines sample size for nonprobability studies based on a judgment that is informed by prior experience, industry standards, or available resources.

The Assignment

For this section of your project you will provide the details of your sampling plan. This plan should contain the four components described above.

1. *Definition of the population.* Has the population been properly defined in terms of elements, sampling units, extent, and time?

2. *Sampling frame.* Has a sampling frame been identified that is available and proper considering the population?

3. *Sample size.* Has the sample size been arrived at through acceptable procedures? Is it appropriate considering time, cost, and desired precision?

4. *Sampling procedure.* Has a sampling procedure been selected and justified relative to alternative procedures?

Use an appendix to show supporting calculations. One way to present the sample size section is through the use of a table like the following.

H (level of half precision)	s (estimate of standard deviation)	z (confidence level)	n (sample size)	Budget, $ ($X per element)
.020	.5	1.96	2401	
.025	.5	1.96	1537	
.030	.5	1.96	1067	
.035	.5	1.96	784	
.040	.5	1.96		
.045	.5	1.96		

Fill in the table for different levels of H and show the corresponding effect on the sample size. Then clearly explain which sample size you will recommend and why.

CHAPTER 9

Coding and Data Entry Using SPSS

Once you have collected the data, it's time to figure out what the data mean. To analyze the data using a computer, it is necessary to enter the codes for each questionnaire into a data file. There are a number of different ways to enter the data, including the use of spreadsheet software such as Excel, word processing software or a statistical software package such as SPSS. Regardless of how the data inputting is handled, there are a few things you need to know and do to get started.

Entering data directly into a statistical software package is a satisfactory method and one we will follow to help get you started. Whether you use a spreadsheet or a statistical package such as SPSS, there are a few basics that you need to recognize.

- Rows represent the responses of an individual respondent.
- Columns represent a variable or an item on a questionnaire.
- Cells contain the values of a given respondent for a specific item.

Before you enter data into a data file, you'll need to code the data into a form the computer can read. Coding the data merely means that you are assigning a numeric value that represents a given response. As you prepare to enter the data, keep in mind the following guidelines:

1. Assign one variable per column. Never try to locate different variables in the same column.
2. Use only numeric codes, not letters of the alphabet or special characters.
3. For each respondent, provide a respondent identification number. This will be useful when you clean the file later.
4. When a question allows for multiple responses, allow for separate columns for each answer.
5. Use standard codes throughout the questionnaire to indicate "no information." You might decide to code all "don't know" responses as an 8 and "does not apply" as a 9, for example.

With a few of the basics covered, it's time to begin data entry. You can use a spreadsheet such as Excel or a statistical software package such as SPSS. To illustrate the process, we'll use SPSS. Let's assume that you have collected your data, have coded the data, and are now ready to enter it into a new SPSS data file. To do so

1. Open SPSS
2. *Double click* a variable name at the top of the column in the Data view or select *View, Variables*
3. To define a new variable, enter a variable name in a blank row.
4. Repeat the steps described below for each variable in your data set.

Exhibits 9.1.1 and 9.1.2 show a portion of a spreadsheet from two distinct views. Exhibit 9.1.1 shows the variable view. That is the view that is used to define and label each question. Notice that on the bottom left portion of the screen the words *Variable View* are

EXHIBIT 9.1.1
Illustrative Spreadsheet:
SPSS Variable View

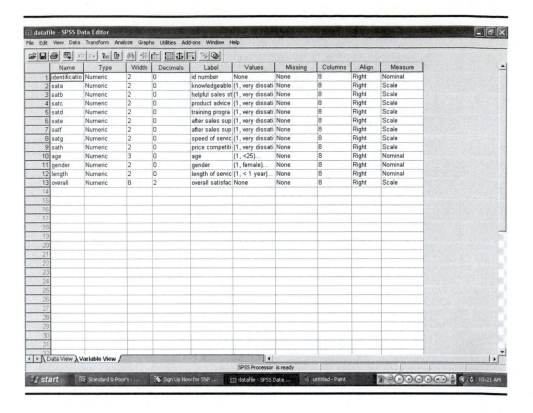

EXHIBIT 9.1.2
Illustrative Spreadsheet:
SPSS Data View

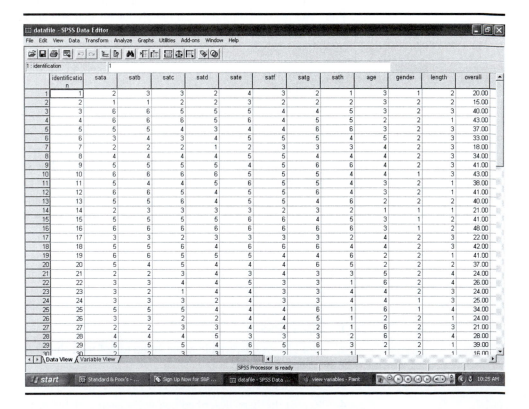

highlighted. You can change back and forth from variable view to *data view* by clicking on the respective buttons at the bottom of the page. Exhibit 9.1.2 shows the data view. This is the window you will use to input data after you have followed the steps described below.

Variable View

Notice in Exhibit 9.1.1 that the variable view includes a number of columns that must be addressed for each question you wish to analyze. The first column (Name) is where you will provide the name for each variable in your data set. There is no need to spend a lot of time thinking about this; just follow the rules described below. You may want to define the name by combining a letter with the question number (q1, q2, q3, etc.).

Variable Names

The following rules apply to variable names:

- The name must begin with a letter.
- Variable names cannot end with a period.
- The length of a name cannot exceed 8 characters (64 in version 12.0).
- Blanks and special characters (!, ?,", and *) cannot be used.
- Each variable name must be unique. Variable names are not case-sensitive.

Variable Type

By default, all new variables are assumed to be numeric. It is likely that this is the variable type you will be using in your project.

1. Click the button in the *Type* cells for the variable you want to define.
2. Select the data type in the *Define Variable Type* box (Exhibit 9.2).

EXHIBIT 9.2

Illustrative Spreadsheet: SPSS Variable Type

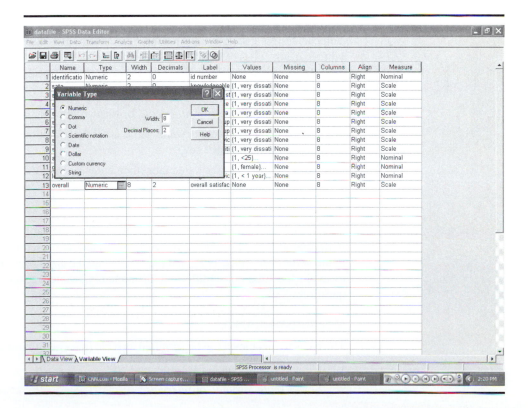

EXHIBIT 9.3

Illustrative Spreadsheet:
SPSS Variable Label

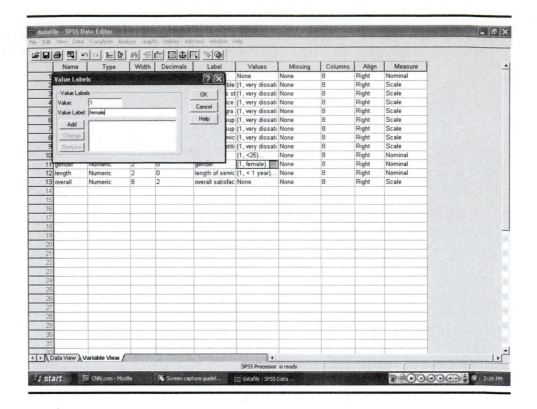

Variable Label

Although variable names can only be 8 characters long, you can describe the variables using labels that can be up to 256 characters long. These descriptive labels are displayed in output, and so you should select a variable label that adequately describes the variable.

Value Label

You can assign descriptive value labels for each coded value in a variable, for example, if you are using codes of 1 and 2 for male and female. Value labels can be up to 60 characters long. In this example, the *value* is the numeric code (1 or 2) and the *value label* describes what the value represents (female or male).

1. Click the button in the *Values* cell for the variable you want to define.

2. For each value, *enter the value and a label.* For example, enter 1 in the Value cell, then Male in the label cell.

3. Click *Add* to enter the value label then enter 2 in the *Value* cell, then Female in the *label* cell, and click *Add.*

4. Click *ok* (Exhibit 9.3).

    If you have a number of questions that utilize the same scale (for example, a Likert scale that utilizes the same value and value label for a series of statements), right click in the *Values* cell, select *copy,* and then *paste* into the appropriate cells. This will enable you to avoid the time-consuming task of manually reentering the value and label for each question.

Measurement Level

The measurement level can be specified as scale (interval or ratio scale), ordinal, or nominal.

1. Click the button in the *Measure* cell.

2. Select *scale, ordinal,* or *interval.*

Entering Data

You can enter data in the data Editor in the data view (Click *View, Data*). You can enter data in any order and can enter by case or by variable.

- The active cell is highlighted.
- The top left corner of the Data Editor displays the variable name and row number of the active cell.
- Data values are recorded when you press Enter or select another cell.
- The cell editor at the top of the Data Editor will display the value for the cell you have selected.
- Entering data in an empty cell will prompt Data Editor to automatically create a new variable with an assigned variable name.

Using SPSS, Excel, or any other statistical package may be intimidating the first time. The brief introduction provided above is intended to help get you started. However, *clicking the Help button* and then *clicking Tutorial* would better serve you. A little time spent with the tutorial will save you many hours in the long run.

CHAPTER 10

Basic Data Analysis

Throughout the semester you have been working on an applied marketing research project. With the data collected, edited, coded, and entered, it is now time for analysis. Before you use some of the sophisticated data analysis methods that are covered in your textbook, you need to summarize the data. It's time to find out what your data mean, and to do that there are some basic statistical methods that you can use as a means of summarizing your results. Later, based on the type of data, the research design, and the needs of the client, you may decide to use more sophisticated techniques.

In this chapter we will examine basic data analysis methods using SPSS. Students generally find that the toughest part of using a software package such as SPSS is getting started. Before we begin with data analysis, it will be productive to recall what you learned during your coverage of measurement about the differences between the types of data: the nominal, ordinal, interval, and ratio scales. The techniques you use will be based on the types of data you have collected.

Measurement Scales

Recall from earlier in the semester your discussion of levels of measurement: nominal, ordinal, interval, and ratio. You learned that these scales have different inherent meanings and that analysis that may be appropriate for one type of scale would be inappropriate for another. Of course, you have an intuitive feel for the different types of appropriate analysis, but it is worthwhile to review.

The *nominal scale* is used to categorize objects. For example, assume we have asked respondents the color of their eyes and have assigned the following numbers to represent different eye colors:

1 = blue eyes

2 = brown eyes

3 = green eyes

4 = hazel eyes

Does it make sense to draw any conclusions based on the assigned numbers? For instance, could we say that since $2 > 1$, brown eyes are somehow more preferable than blue? Could we say that the average eye color is 2.4 and interpret that in some way? Of course not. Common sense tells us that the only finding that would be reasonable to report would be the number of individuals with each eye color and that the only measure of central tendency that would have meaning would be the mode. The same holds true when we are using a scale to categorize individuals by gender or by ethnic origin or any time we are using an arbitrary assignment of numbers to represent a given categorization scheme.

Since the data are nominal, it is only permissible to report the number and percentage of those with each eye color and state that there are more of one color than the others.

The *ordinal scale* is a more powerful scale because the assigned numbers reflect order as well as classification. You may use this scale if you ask consumers to rank brands from most preferred to least, for example. If a consumer ranks one brand as the most preferred and a second brand as the second most preferred, you know that the first is preferred to the second. However, you don't know if the difference in preference between the first and second is the same as between the second and third. You may have used a five-point Likert scale, for example, in which respondents are asked to indicate their level of agreement with a number of statements. This scale and most marketing measures reflect ordinal measurements. The appropriate measure of central tendency is the median.

The *interval scale* demonstrates the properties of the two previous scales—classification and order—and also the distance property. That is, the researcher can demonstrate the differences between each pair of scale points. Often in marketing, a series of ordinal questions are transformed by summing the responses to create an interval scale. For example, if questions 5 through 9 measure customer satisfaction with a given attribute, it is good and common practice to create a new variable for each respondent in the database which would be the average of the respondents' scores on those questions (see "Transforming Variables" later in this chapter). In this situation the new variable would be treated as an interval scale. The mean, median, and mode are appropriate measures of central tendency for interval scale data.

The *ratio scale* has a natural zero point so that we can compare the absolute magnitude of two data points: "Someone who makes $100,000 makes twice as much as someone who earns $50,000." Normally the ratio scale requests respondents to respond with a specific value to questions such as "What is your current age?" or "In the past seven days how many times did you shop in the downtown shopping district?" All statistics appropriate for the interval scale are appropriate for the ratio scale.

There is a long-standing debate among researchers who believe that most marketing measurements are ordinal and those who argue that such scales can be treated as interval measures for purposes of data analysis. There is sufficient evidence to support both sides, and your instructor probably will guide you on this issue.

The above discussion was presented as a review and a reminder. Before you conduct an analysis of a given variable, you need to consider the nature of that variable and decide on the appropriate treatment.

Descriptive Statistics

Once the data are ready for analysis, there are some basic statistical procedures that you will want to perform. The first step for many research projects is to summarize the data, to take the many individual responses and attempt to determine what they all mean. With a statistical software package such as SPSS this is a relatively easy task. Before you begin to generate numerous pages of output, however, take some time to consider your objectives. Your analysis must be linked to the questions the study is meant to answer. Generating dozens of pages of statistical output without regard to the research objectives and without proper interpretation is a common mistake in student projects.

You may want to start by producing frequency counts for many of your questions. This will provide the number who responded for each category as well as the percentage in each category and the cumulative percentages.

Exhibit 10.1 presents a summary of steps used in SPSS to generate a frequency table. In a study of satisfaction with a retail vendor, a six-point scale was used to measure the degree of satisfaction with after-sales support. The results are shown in Table 10.1.

While the procedure detailed above includes statistics along with each frequency table, you can generate descriptive statistics without generating frequency tables by using the following steps. The output will include the number of valid responses, the minimum and maximum values, the mean, and the standard deviation.

To generate descriptive statistics in SPSS:

1. Select *Analyze*.

2. Select *Descriptive Statistics*.

3. Select *Descriptives*.

4. Move the selected variables to the *Variables* box by marking the variable and clicking the *right arrow*.

5. Select *OK*.

EXHIBIT 10.1

Generating a Frequency
Table in SPSS

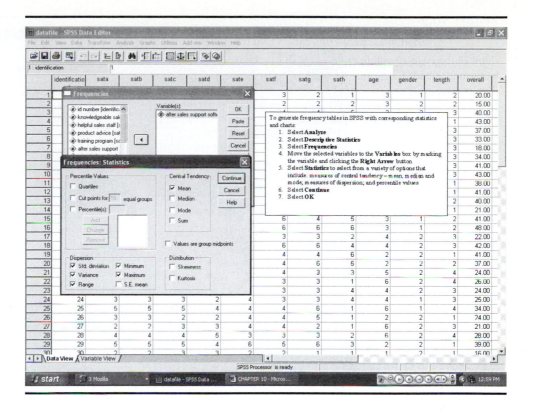

TABLE 10.1 Frequencies

Statistics		
after-sales support software		
N	Valid	50
	Missing	0
Mean		3.82
Median		4.00
Standard deviation		1.289
Minimum		1
Maximum		6

Frequencies

		Frequency	Percent	Valid Percent	Cumulative Percent
		after-sales support software			
Valid	Very dissatisfied	3	6.0	6.0	6.0
	Dissatisfied	4	8.0	8.0	14.0
	Slightly dissatisfied	12	24.0	24.0	38.0
	Slightly satisfied	15	30.0	30.0	68.0
	Satisfied	12	24.0	24.0	92.0
	Very satisfied	4	8.0	8.0	100.0
	Total	50	100.0	100.0	

Charts

It's a good idea to use graphics to give the reader a quick and easy insight into the information that is being presented. It often is said that a picture is worth a thousand words. That can be especially true when an effective graphic displays complex information in a way

EXHIBIT 10.2

Generating a Bar Chart in SPSS

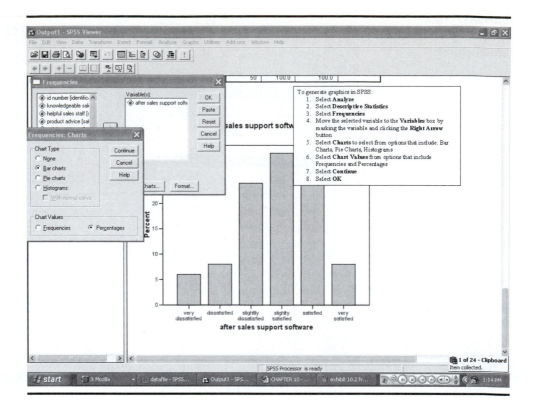

that contributes significantly to the communication process between researcher and client. Generating bar charts, pie charts, or histograms is easily done using most statistical software packages. Exhibit 10.2 shows how to generate a chart in SPSS and presents a bar chart for the satisfaction with after-sales support question that was discussed earlier.

Cross-Tabulations

Whereas *frequency tabulations* look at one variable at a time and are the result of a simple process of counting the number of cases that are classified in a certain way, *cross-tabulations* consider two variables simultaneously, categorizing the number of respondents who have answered two or more questions. Cross-tabulations are very useful when one is looking for relationships between two or more variables and are especially useful when one is looking for differences among subgroups. Cross-tabulations are typically the major form of data analysis used in marketing research projects. Well-developed cross-tabulations can be a powerful tool that allows the researcher to study relationships between variables and explain those relationships to clients in a clear and concise manner. Exhibit 10.3 shows how to generate a cross-tabulation in SPSS.

Cross-tabulations examine relationships between pairs of nominal or ordinal variables. Relationships between interval or ratio variables may be measured using correlations and regressions. Cross-tabs are used when the researcher wants to find out how one variable is affected by the value of another variable. For example, suppose a technology vendor was interested in learning whether there were differences among males and females in terms of satisfaction with after-sales support for software. In other words, does membership in one group, (male or female) allow one to predict whether a person is likely to be satisfied. Table 10.2 presents SPSS output showing the cross tabulation of two variables: gender and satisfaction. When generating a cross-tabulation, always compute the percentages in the direction of the presumed causal variable. In this case we hypothesized that gender may influence level of satisfaction.

Calculating percentages should always be shown as above, that is, in the direction of the causal factor. The determination of which variable is the causal variable should take into account the probability that membership in one group is likely to be affected by membership

EXHIBIT 10.3

Generating Cross-
Tabulations in SPSS

in the other. It makes sense that one's level of satisfaction is affected by one's gender, but the level of satisfaction would not affect one's gender.

Note that the significance level (*p* value) of .000 under the label "Asymp.Sig. (2-sided)" in the output implies that the chances of getting a chi-square value as high as 12.347 when there is no relationship between gender and satisfaction is less than 1 in 1,000. The relationship between gender and satisfaction is unlikely to have occurred by chance. In other words, it appears that the vendor has a real problem with his or her female customers.

TABLE 10.2 Case Processing Summary

	Cases					
	Valid		Missing		Total	
	N	Percent	*N*	Percent	*N*	Percent
Gender* satisfaction with software sales	50	100.0	0	.0	50	100.0

Gender* Satisfaction with Software Sales Cross-Tabulation

			Satisfaction with Software Sales		
			Dissatisfied	Satisfied	Total
Gender	Female	Count	20	2	22
		% within gender	90.9%	9.1%	100.0%
	Male	Count	12	16	28
		% within gender	42.9%	57.1%	100.0%
Total		Count	32	18	50
		% within gender	64.0%	36.0%	100.0%

(Continued)

TABLE 10.2 Case Processing Summary *(Continued)*

Chi-Square Tests

	Value	df	Asymptotic Significance (2-sided)	Exact Significance (2-sided)	Exact Significance (1-sided)
Pearson chi-square	12.347[†]	1	.000		
Continuity Correction*	10.349	1	.001		
Likelihood ratio	13.695	1	.000		
Fisher's exact test				.001	.000
Linear-by-linear Association	12.100	1	.001		
No valid cases	50				

*Computed only for a 2 × 2 table.

[†]0 cells (.0%) have expected count less than 5. The minimum expected count is 7.92.

Transforming Variables

When dealing with survey data, you often will find that it makes sense to create a new variable from a combination of variables. In this chapter we have used an example showing customers' satisfaction with the level of after-sales support for new software. In the same study there were questions that measured satisfaction with the vendor on a number of dimensions. If the vendor was interested in combining these scores to come up with an overall satisfaction score, he or she could do that by using the *Transform* function of SPSS to create a new variable. Exhibit 10.4 shows the steps you need to follow to create a new variable and the SPSS screen.

EXHIBIT 10.4

Transforming Raw Data into a New Variable

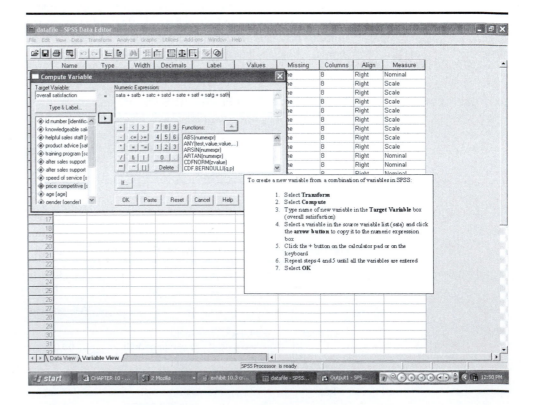

EXHIBIT 10.5

Recoding a Variable

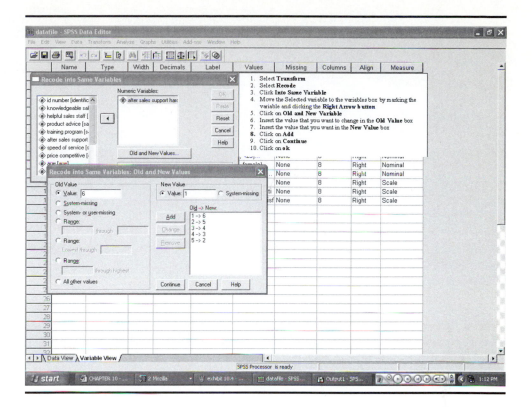

Recoding a Variable

Sometimes you may want to recode a variable. Perhaps you have worded a Likert scale statement negatively so that agreement would indicate a negative attitude for the particular question, as opposed to the rest of the statements, in which agreement would indicate a positive attitude. To recode a variable into the same variable follow the steps shown in Exhibit 10.5.

Summary

This chapter has reviewed the basic scales used in measurement. You were reminded of the appropriate analysis for each scale (nominal, ordinal, interval, and ratio) and instructed to consider the nature of any data that you collect before you begin data analysis. Basic methods of data analysis were reviewed, with attention given to the specific steps necessary to use SPSS to run frequency tables, descriptive statistics, charts, cross-tabulations, and transformations. The methods covered in this chapter are commonly used techniques in marketing research and should provide the basics you need to conduct your data analysis. For more advanced methods of data analysis, consult the tutorial that is provided with your statistical package.

CHAPTER 11

The Written Report

Every major marketing research textbook includes a chapter on the written marketing research report. While each of these texts provides a slightly different recommended format, the differences are not significant. Your professor may recommend the format described in your text or a similar one tied to a grading rubric that will be used in your course. There is no single standard format, but there are components that should be included in every research report. This chapter will review those components and relate them to the score sheet that was provided in Appendix 1C. In the end, however, every research report will be unique in some way, responding to different client needs and different research objectives.

Regardless of the format you use, the goal of the written report is the same: to communicate the results of your project in a clear, concise, and complete fashion. A quality report will enhance your credibility and provide the reader with a clear understanding of the results and the methods and procedures used to generate those results. Outstanding work on the various stages of the research project can be negated by a poorly written and carelessly edited written report. As you develop the report, keep in mind that you may need to communicate with more than one audience. Your professor may be interested in the technical components of your project, looking to assess your knowledge and progress and your efforts and contributions to the project, as well as the final results. Your client will be more interested in understanding the results and drawing action-oriented conclusions from the study. Writing for multiple audiences is a challenge that regularly faces marketing researchers. As you prepare the final report, keep in mind the interests of your audiences. If your instructor has indicated that a given grading rubric will be utilized, refer to it often. That rubric will indicate the format and the levels of emphasis your instructor prefers.

If your report is intended for a client, its primary purpose will be to communicate the findings of the project. The report must relate the findings back to the original research objectives and provide a clear interpretation of the findings. A challenge that all researchers face is credibility. A report that is well written, carefully edited, organized, and accurate demonstrates the researcher's attention to detail and enhances his or her credibility. Do not let the substance of the research project be lost because of careless style.

Format of the Written Report

1. Title page
2. Table of contents
3. Executive summary
4. Introduction: review of the decision situation (assignment from Chapter 3)
5. Body
    a. Research objectives (Chapter 4 assignment)
    b. Review of literature (Chapter 5 assignment)
    c. Research methods and procedures (Chapter 6 assignment)
    d. Sampling plan (Chapter 8 assignment)
6. Data analysis and findings
7. Conclusions
8. Limitations

9. Appendixes
   a.   Questionnaire (Chapter 7 assignment)
   b.   Calculations used to determine sample size (Chapter 8 assignment)
   c.   Detailed statistical tables
10. References

Title Page

The title page should include the following:

- The title of the project, which should clearly describe the nature of the study and the client, for example, "Patrons' Customer Satisfaction with Canale's Restaurant"
- The client's name
- The names of the group members
- The section number and the name of the instructor
- The date the project was turned in

Table of Contents

The table of contents includes the specific sections of the report in the order in which they appear, with appendixes and bibliography and appropriate page numbers. Subheadings within each section usually are included with the page number, although they may be omitted. The table of contents should include the lists of tables and figures with page numbers as well.

Executive Summary

The executive summary provides the major points of the report in summary form. In many cases the executive summary is the only part of the report that the busy executive will read. The summary should provide the reader with a brief background in order to better understand the study's results and conclusions. It should outline the purpose of the study, the research problems that guided the research, and the key findings related to each research problem. Conclusions based on the evidence identified in the body of the report should be included. Whether you include a set of recommendations based on your findings will depend on your situation. Some managers prefer to determine the course of action themselves and are not interested in the researcher's recommendations. Others believe the researcher is in the best position to interpret the findings and make a recommendation.

Introduction: Review of the Decision Situation

The introduction provides a review of the situation facing decision makers, providing the reader with the information needed to understand the total report. Relevant background information that provides insights into the decision problem should be provided. Background on the company, a description of the major competitors, and a review of the relevant industry information should place the situation faced by decision makers in the proper perspective. The depth of this analysis will depend on the familiarity of the reader with the situation. Your instructor may require more depth in this section than the client typically would. In general, the more diverse the audiences are, the more extensive this section should be.

The introduction should state the objectives of the research and the rationale for the research project. As you prepare this section, keep in mind that its purpose is to familiarize readers with the situation so that they will be better able to appreciate the body of the report.

This section should introduce and define the terms that will be used later. Define the competitors and brands that are included in any discussion of market share. Describe the geographic boundaries of a given market or the kinds of information that typically will be sought in this type of study. For example, in a brand usage study management may want top of mind awareness (first mention), unaided brand awareness (top three mentions), an evaluation of the advertising, and several other items. Describing each of these is important to the effective communication of the report results.

The introduction may provide history, but it should be relevant to the present situation. You don't need to trace the company back to its founding. What is appropriate for a company's Web site is not necessarily appropriate for this report. The history should relate to the circumstances that led to the present situation.

Body

Research Objectives and Information Needs   The *research objectives* need to be stated explicitly. The research objectives specify what you want to know when the study has been completed. They should be listed and stated in terms of the knowledge to be gained.

The *information needs* are a detailed breakdown of the research objectives. Chapter 4 provides some good examples of both research objectives and information needs.

This section is important because it describes the information gathered for the study. It gives the reader a basis for an evaluation of the questionnaire and ultimately the success of the project. There should be no discrepancy between the information that ultimately is gathered, analyzed, and reported and the objectives stated in this section.

Literature Review   This is a section that typically would not be included in a marketing research report, and your instructor may advise you to omit it. It is included here because of the unique educational objectives of the student marketing research project. For the purposes of this project, the literature review is intended to serve as a summary of the methodological approaches generally associated with the particular type of study used in your project. If your study is designed to measure customer satisfaction, your review should focus on customer satisfaction studies that have been published. In those studies, the authors will have defined the relevant terms, described the methodology that was employed and the measures that were used, and provided a summary of the findings.

The literature review should include the following sections:

1. Conceptual definition
2. Methodology
3. Measures

Research Methodology   This section is intended to communicate the specific methods that were used in the project. Specifically, this section should address the following:

1. What research design was used: exploratory, descriptive, or causal?
2. What were the secondary sources of data that were utilized?
3. What were the procedures used to collect primary data (observation or questioning), and what was the method of contact (mail, online, telephone, personal)?

Sampling Plan   This section may be more technical than what your client wants, but your instructor will be very interested in it. This section should include the following information:

1. A definition of the population in terms of the element, sampling unit, extent, and time.
2. A description of the sampling frame. How was the list generated, and what are the characteristics of the list?
3. How was the sample size determined? The specific calculations should be included in an appendix.
4. What sampling procedure has been utilized? Why has this procedure been used?

Data Analysis and Findings

The actual findings of your study will be presented in this section. Your findings should be described with supporting tables and charts. The findings should be arranged to match up with each research objective. Remember, your research objective is a statement of what you want to know when the study has been completed; this section is your opportunity to show that you have met those objectives. An important aspect of this section is the interpretation of the findings that are provided to management. The interpretation of the results should be objective and based on the findings.

Frequency tables, cross-tabulations, and descriptive statistics should be presented in a way that addresses specific research questions. More sophisticated analysis techniques may need to be accompanied with a brief description of the rationale for their use and an interpretation of their meaning. Highly technical or complex charts that may be more difficult to understand may be included in an appendix.

If your project was a proposal rather than a full-scale study, you should include the mock-up tables that indicate the analysis that would be run if the study were to be conducted. Relate the mock-up tables to the research objectives as you would if they were data tables.

Conclusions

The research objectives were a statement of what management wished to know as a result of the project. The conclusion section should summarize the findings from various tables and charts in a way that addresses the research objective. The conclusions are derived from the findings and can be considered generalizations that address questions related to the research objectives.

Limitations

No study is perfect, and yours won't be. Though you have made every effort to comply with best practices, certain factors will conspire to place limitations on your project. The limitations may be nonsampling errors related to nonresponse or the sampling frame or any number of other common limitations. It is important that the researcher acknowledge the limitations and inform the reader. This section should mention only the limitations that could truly affect and bias the findings and explain the possible impact. You do not need to offer a generic description of every possible factor that could limit your study. Rather, focus on those which are most problematic. This section addresses the credibility of the researcher. It is much better for the researcher to present the limitations than to have the reader discover them later.

Appendixes

The appendixes include detailed information that complements the body of the report. Include the questionnaire, sample size calculations, a detailed statistical analysis, and the schedule.

A Few Final Thoughts

Throughout this semester, you have been working on an applied marketing research project in a stepwise manner. In each of several chapters of this manual you have been given an assignment that represents a significant step in the research process. You may have received feedback from your instructor on each of these assignments, perhaps causing you to revise that portion of the project. As you prepare the final written report, your task will be to integrate the assignment pieces into a coherent unified document. This will require some careful editing and attention to detail to ensure that the various parts are consistent with one another and that the writing style is also consistent.

A common problem in student projects is report "padding." Students often include pages of tables and computer output in a shotgun approach, apparently hoping that the longer the report, the greater the evidence of effort. An indiscriminate inclusion of tables and output detracts from the final report and should be avoided. Likewise, the inclusion of tables or figures that are not referenced in the text gives the appearance of a data dump and distracts the reader from the major findings of the study. Remember, when your instructor advises you to be concise, he or she means it. Report on the major findings that are related to the original research objectives, not on every conceivable cross-tabulation you have run.

One final suggestion is in regard to the editing process. You may decide that each member of the team will be responsible for editing his or her work. While that is certainly necessary, experience has shown that teams that select a student member to serve as the "editor in chief" generally produce superior written reports. This editor should pay particular attention to inconsistencies and redundancies that may be the result of individual students writing selected parts of the report. For example, it would not be appropriate to claim in the methodology section that a personal interview would be conducted, only to contradict that when discussing the questionnaire by suggesting that it would be administered via telephone. Likewise, it would not be appropriate to repeat key information in each section, a common problem when multiple authors do not coordinate their work.

While the editor plays a crucial role, the final report is the responsibility of each member of the group. Accordingly, each should review the report after the editor has completed his or her work and before it is submitted to the instructor. A final review meeting may be necessary to resolve any problems that are raised by individual members.